TEAM-BASED ORGANIZATIONS
Developing a Successful Team Environment

TEAM-BASED ORGANIZATIONS
Developing a Successful Team Environment

James H. Shonk

BUSINESS ONE IRWIN
Homewood, Illinois 60430

© JAMES H. SHONK, 1992

This publication is designed to provide accurate and authoritative information in regard to the subject matter covered. It is sold with the understanding that neither the author nor the publisher is engaged in rendering legal, accounting, or other professional service. If legal advice or other expert assistance is required, the services of a competent professional person should be sought.

From a Declaration of Principles jointly adopted by a Committee of the American Bar Association and a Committee of Publishers.
Sponsoring editor: Cynthia A. Zigmund
Project editor: Rebecca Dodson
Production manager: Mary Jo Parke
Compositor: Eastern Graphics
Typeface: 11/14 Palatino
Printer: Arcata Graphics/Kingsport

Library of Congress Cataloging-in-Publication Data

Shonk, James H.
    Team-based organizations : developing a successful team environment / James H. Shonk.
      p.   cm.
    Includes bibliographical references and index.
    ISBN 1-55623-703-0
    1. Work groups—Management. I. Title.
HD66.S56 1992
658.4'036—dc20   91–32220

Printed in the United States of America
   3 4 5 6 7 8 9 0 AGK 9 8 7 6 5 4 3 2

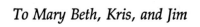

To Mary Beth, Kris, and Jim

Preface

In 1969, Beckhard wrote about the constant need for organizations to seek new ways of organizing—ways that would fully utilize their human resources to effectively meet the challenges of the environment.[1] During the 1970s and into the 1980s, managers began to realize that traditional organizational structures, such as functional or departmental organizations, were not always able to respond to marketplace demands. Many organizations began looking for better ways to use their human resources and to improve collaboration. Furthermore, organizations were struggling with a seeming lack of commitment or work ethic within their work forces and were losing the quality battle to imports.

To address these issues, many organizations partially turned to teams. They formed quality circles or started quality of work life, as well as efforts in employee involvement or employee participation efforts. All of these approaches were aimed at giving employees more influence over decisions and at increasing collaboration among various skills, disciplines, and levels.

---

[1] Richard Beckhard, *Organization Development: Strategies and Models* (Reading, Mass.: Addison-Wesley Publishing, 1969), p. *v*.

These organizations discovered that teams offered an effective way to coordinate across organizational boundaries in solving problems and in gaining employee commitment. As a result, more and more organizations turned toward teams to better accomplish their goals.

Much has been written on developing and managing a team (see Dyer, Hirschhorn, and Shonk).[2] However, little attention has been given to how to plan for and manage the transition of an organization from a traditional hierarchical and functional structure to an organization built around teams.

This book, *Team-Based Organizations*, is about organizing in new ways: It is about organizing around teams to support an interdependence that already exists. The nature of the modern business enterprise is such that the interdependence of its parts is increasing in response to a more complex environment, one requiring many skills and functions to effectively compete.

Traditional organizational structures and processes often work against effective interdependency by focusing on individuals and tightly bound functions or units. New structures and processes must be developed to more effectively manage a firm's interdependencies. Many firms are finding that team-based organizations are a very promising strategy for managing these interdependencies.

This book is the result of my consulting experiences while helping firms manage the transition to a team-based organization. It is written to give managers an understanding of their role and the issues and processes involved in making the transition. The emphasis is upon changing existing organizations, but the concepts apply as well to new organizations (for more infor-

---

[2] William G. Dyer, *Team Building: Issues and Alternatives* (Reading, Mass.: Addison-Wesley Publishing, 1977).   Larry Hirschhorn, *Managing in the New Team Environment* (Reading, Mass.: Addison-Wesley Publishing, 1991).   James H. Shonk, *Working in Teams* (New York: Amacom, 1982). Now published by The Team Center, 21 Sarah Bishop Road, Ridgefield, Connecticut.

mation on creating new team-based organizations, see Lawler, Walton, and Cherry).[3]

The material in this book is intended for managers who want to build more effective organization-wide teamwork, for organizational development, and training professionals and students in organizational behavior curriculums. Many of the processes that have proven successful in practice within General Foods and with such clients as Ford Motor Company, General Electric, GTE, and Sherwin Williams are presented to provide information on what other organizations have done. I also have presented many of the pitfalls, so the reader I hope can avoid them.

Some of the processes presented and the issues identified might not fit your organization's unique character. Don't be overly concerned if your organization does not meet all the criteria and conditions presented to effectively launch teams. Rather, recognize that the issues may need to be addressed at some point, and they frequently can be resolved only over a long time. This book is intended to provide information to stimulate your thinking; it is not intended to be used as a cookbook but as a tool in determining what is best for your organization.

Although I have a bias toward participative teams as an effective means of accomplishing work, this book is not written to convince you to use teams. You will have to assess whether a team-based organization is right for your firm. If you decide to increase your use of teams, I hope the ideas presented will help you achieve your goals.

---

[3] Edward E. Lawler III, *High Involvement Management* (San Francisco: Jossey Bass, 1986).   Richard Walton, "How to Counter Alienation in the Plant," *Harvard Business Review*, November–December 1972, pp. 70–81.   Richard L. Cherry, *The Development of General Motors' Team-Based Plants, the Innovative Organization: Productivity Programs in Action* (New York: Pergamon Press, 1982), (7) pp. 125–48.

How to Use This Book

Chapter One, "Teams," defines the meaning of team and team-based organizations. It presents the origins and impact of teams within the United States to show how team-based organizations have been successful in improving organizational productivity and employee job satisfaction. The chapter also discusses the advantages and disadvantages of teams. Finally, Chapter One identifies the keys to a successful change effort, so the reader will identify how they are incorporated into the planning and implementation processes.

Chapter Two, "Are Teams Right for Your Organization?," shows managers how to determine where teams already exist in their organization. It identifies the factors and analyses that go into deciding to organize around teams and how to determine if increasing the use of teams is appropriate. The chapter also discusses the issues that may make it difficult to create a team-based organization.

Chapter Three, "Types of Teams," reviews the different types and how they impact upon the organization, based on their autonomy. It explores the relationship between teams, participation, and organizational structure and discusses when to use each type of team.

Chapter Four, "Organizational Support for Teams," explains how participative teams affect the organization's structure and processes. It explains how to avoid merely plugging a team into an existing organization without expecting the organization to change. Chapter Four also shows how structures and processes can be altered to be supportive of teams.

Chapter Five, "Getting Started," identifies the various issues for which managers will need to plan while starting a team-based change effort. It provides examples of what other organizations have done, and it includes planning guidelines. Chapter Five explores how to overcome resistance, as well as identifying the issues that unions and management need to discuss before beginning. Finally, the chapter provides criteria for determining the start-up area.

Chapter Six, "Organization Evolution," describes two approaches to change: evolution and redesign. The approaches are not mutually exclusive but are separated, to better explain each. The chapter describes the evolution process and how other companies have used a parallel organization, including the roles and relationships of parallel organization committees.

Chapter Seven, "Designing a Team-Based Organization," shows how to create a design team to redesign the organization around teams; it also provides guidelines and criteria for the redesign. And it outlines the role of the core group and the design team.

Chapter Eight, "Training," describes the types of training typically needed to support a greater use of teams, including the audience, purpose, and content for each type.

Chapter Nine, "Leading a Team-Based Organization," describes the role of a team leader and management's role in managing the transition to a team-based organization. It identifies major issues for managers to address to perpetuate the organization's success.

Chapter Ten, "Keys to Success," summarizes the keys to a successful team-based change effort and pulls together the concepts and techniques presented throughout the book.

JAMES H. SHONK

Acknowledgments

I wish to thank Patricia Floyd, Kelley Gordon, Anne Harris, Colly Holmes, and Don Reek, who were very helpful with their editorial comments and ideas for a workbook that spawned this book's first draft.

Its next iteration was the result of input from many friends and colleagues—Ed Lawler, Dick Axelrod, Bob DuBrul, and Jim Stillwell.

Ed Schein and Dick Beckhard were very helpful with their editorial suggestions and ideas on the flow of the book and how to make it easier to understand.

Joan Mannion and Barbara Milne assisted with several drafts, and helped with editing.

Mary Beth and Kris provided editing and support.

Thank you all! Your contributions are greatly appreciated.

Contents

Chapter One

Teams

WHAT CONSTITUTES A TEAM?

A team is "two or more people who must coordinate their activities to accomplish a common goal."[1] The common goal and the required coordination make them a team. It is not enough for people to want to coordinate because it would be nice. Coordination must be required to accomplish the task in order to be a team.[2]

With this definition of a team, it is easy to see that much of the work of large, complex organizations is performed by teams.

Given that most organizations consist of a number of teams, the challenge facing managers is not whether to use teams but *how* to most effectively use teams. As a manager you will need to know what type of teams to create, how to organize to support teamwork, how to make the transition to greater teamwork, and how to manage an enterprise that is organized around teams.

---

[1] Mark Plovnick, Ronald Fry, and Irwin Rubin, "New Developments in O.D. Technology: Programmed Team Development," *Training and Development Journal*, April 4, 1975.

[2] James H. Shonk, *Working in Teams* (New York: Amacom Press, 1982). Second printing by The Team Center, a division of Shonk & Associates, Ridgefield, Connecticut.

TEAM-BASED ORGANIZATIONS

Companies generally are organized around individuals, functions, or departments as the basic work unit. A team-based organization is one that uses a team as its basic work unit. Teams do much of the planning, decision making, and implementation within the work setting.

In some organizations, teams do much of the work that typically would be handled by several functions. For example, in team-based facilities, teams are responsible for a wide range of activities—ranging from receiving materials, to manufacturing, to warehousing.

In more traditional organizations, these activities typically are handled by different departments. Teams also perform many of the functions often handled by staff groups, such as hiring, training, and financial analysis.

ORIGIN OF TEAM-BASED ORGANIZATIONS

The proponents of socio-technical systems have been the forerunners in designing jobs to meet both the social needs of the individual as well as the technical needs of the organization. The proponents advocated the use of teams as the basic work unit in their designs of early team-based organizations. Eric Trist was one of the forerunners of this work, which dates back to experiments in coal mines as early as 1951.[3]

The groundwork established by Trist and other early socio-technical advocates led to the development of team-based organizations in the 60s and 70s by such companies as Procter & Gamble and General Foods. These organizations used teams as the basic work unit and designed the rest of the organization to be supportive of team efforts.

The success of these early efforts started a parade of companies organizing around teams. Some organizations that have been

---

[3] E. L. Trist and K. W. Bamforth, "Some Social Psychological Consequences of the Long Wall Method of Coal-Getting," *Human Relations* 4 (1951), pp. 3–38.

using work teams are Cummins Engine, 1973; Digital Equipment Corporation, 1982; Textronix, 1983; General Electric, 1985; LTV Steel, 1985; Champion International, 1985; Caterpillar, 1986; Boeing, 1987; A. O. Smith, 1987.[4]

The successes that organizations had with teams in the 70s and 80s led to a widespread realization that organizing around teams is not a fad but, given the right circumstances, can be a more effective way to perform work than the traditional functional and hierarchical organization. The advantages of teams and functional organizations will be reviewed more thoroughly in Chapters Two and Three.

WHY TEAM-BASED ORGANIZATIONS?

The two basic reasons that companies organize around teams are to empower employees to more fully contribute and to increase organizational productivity.

They go together. It is not a matter of either/or. The main value of teams is their ability to assemble and empower employees to use their talents to improve the organization. In more fully participating in decisions and planning how work will be performed, employee contribution and, for most, job satisfaction are increased.

Companies turn more and more to teams because old structures do not adequately respond to marketplace demands or because they see teams as a better way of doing business. There are several specific reasons given by organizations for going to teams, which are subsets of productivity and employee contribution.

Quality

The competition from abroad and the pressure by consumers for quality products and services has spawned an increased emphasis on quality. A credit services company found that its func-

---

[4] "The Payoff from Teamwork," *Business Week*, July 10, 1989, pp. 56–62.

tional organization was not providing the quality of service it wanted. When customers called, they were transferred to various functions to provide the service.

The company has organized into multi-functional teams that focus on specific customers. Employees are being trained to perform several functions to greatly reduce the number of times a customer call is transferred and to provide faster and higher-quality service.

Flexibility

The rapid changes in the business environment of the past two decades, such as rapidly expanding computer technology, the influx of foreign competition, and the economic contractions and expansions, have made it very clear that organizations of the future must be flexible. They must be able to adapt to rapid changes in the environment.

The research division of a company went from a functional to a team-based organization for several reasons, one of which was to flexibly deploy resources. The company formed multi-functional teams, drawing together the several disciplines needed for a project. One of these teams discontinued a project, when it showed little promise, 6 to 12 months before the manager said the project would have been stopped under the old functional organization. The employees on the team were easily deployed to new projects.

This organization has put together teams in response to several key business challenges and disbands them when finished. Employees allocate their time to more than one team; and the directors who support several teams are charged with establishing the priorities for projects and allocating the resources of finished projects to new ones.

Coordination

When I talk with managers, one of the things they mention as being a difficult task is coordinating the efforts of the various functions to work well together. Many organizations have formed teams of representatives from the various functions and have pushed the coordination responsibility down to the team.

For example, Ford advertises that teams help in the planning and production of its automobiles. One company pulls together teams composed of people from research, development, manufacturing, and marketing to take products from the idea stage to the marketplace.

(4) Employee Satisfaction and Development

By empowering employees to plan their work and make decisions, organizations are finding that talents are emerging and developing that previously were neither recognized nor utilized.

In a manufacturing facility, when it asked for volunteers to start a newsletter, it got 70 volunteers and a first-class newsletter. Another organization is using members of its design team to conduct team training. Employees who have worked in team settings are being sought to transfer and help other parts of the organization.

(5) Productivity/Cost

Considerable data exist that suggest teams can be an effective method to meet organizational goals, productivity, and cost reduction. A few examples follow.

At one point, General Foods compared its Topeka pet food plant—a newly designed team-based facility—to one of its traditional plants that manufactured a similar product. The company found Topeka to be roughly 30 percent more productive. This included lower overhead costs as well as productivity increases. At the same time, attitude surveys of employees were conducted and compared to other innovative, high-involvement organizations. The Topeka employees scored higher on all but one of the questions.

A study by the New York Stock Exchange Office of Economic Research asked corporations with 500 or more employees which of the many efforts they have undertaken to improve productivity have had the most impact.[5] Thirty-two percent of those surveyed mentioned teams.

Furthermore, many of the other activities that were highly rated are responsibilities typically taken on by teams. For example, in teams, employees are involved in setting company objectives, establishing work hours, structuring the manufacturing facilities and office space, working on task forces, scheduling the work flow, doing their own appraisals, and receiving performance feedback. These items were mentioned in the survey as having had a positive impact on productivity.

A GE plant in Salisbury, North Carolina typically changes product models a dozen times a day by using a team system to produce lighting panel-boards. This plant has increased productivity by 250 percent, compared with other General Electric plants that produce the same products. Shenendoah Life Insurance Company has reduced employee-to-supervisor ratios from 7 to 1 to about 37 to 1.[6]

Ford started experimenting with teams in the late 1970s and early 1980s. A problem-solving team of production workers in the Ford Dearborn Glass plant took on work normally assigned to outside contractors, at an estimated savings of $500,000, and it significantly shortened the time normally required for project completion.

In 1971, Motorola claimed turnover was down 25 percent, productivity was up 30 percent, and attendance had increased to 95 percent due to the use of a team philosophy. This philosophy of managing used the creativity of the individual and of the team collectively to effect solutions through consultative and involvement techniques.

The team effort at Motorola began when an assembly line was staffed with new operators who were to build complicated radio receivers. When many problems were encountered and the line

---

[5] William M. Batten, chairman, New York Stock Exchange, *People and Productivity—A Challenge to Corporate America* (New York Stock Exchange Office of Economic Research, November 1982).

[6] John J. Sherwood, "Creating Work Cultures with Competitive Advantage," *Organizational Dynamics*, American Management Association, 1988, pp. 5–27.

was about to be shut down, engineers and supervisors went to work to find the solution, but to little avail. By involving the assembly line workers, many of the problems began to be solved.

For example, the workers developed a brush with an air hose on it that removed metallic particles that were causing electrical short circuits. As other problems were solved, the employees began to meet more regularly. They decided they would like to have the responsibility of tracking their own performance. The result was that they developed a method for recognizing the performance of members of the team.[7]

At a recent Ecology of Work Life Conference, a company speaker said that whether manufacturing facilities use a self-managing team approach is a major consideration in determining which plants get new products to manufacture.

ADVANTAGES AND PROBLEMS

Teams are not a cure-all for all ills. However, where interdependencies exist and teamwork offers a competitive advantage, work teams can be an effective way of operating an organization. Lawler, in his *High Involvement Management*, says that:

> Overall, work teams make an important difference in the participative structure of organizations. Individuals end up with knowledge and skills, information, rewards, and power that they do not have in traditional organizations. Thus, work teams are likely to have an important positive impact on organizational effectiveness.

Lawler also lists many areas where effective teams can provide improvement:

1. Improvement is likely in work methods and procedures.
2. A gain is likely in attraction and retention.
3. Staffing flexibility increases.
4. Service and product quality usually increases.
5. Rate of output may improve.
6. Staff support level can be reduced.

---

[7] Brian Hays, "Turnover Decreased, Efficiency Increased, Absenteeism Reduced, Morale Improved with the Motorola Assembly Team," *Assembly Engineering*, July 1971.

7. Supervision can be reduced.
8. Decision making is likely to improve.[8]

Perhaps the greatest advantage of teams is that they put the skills and responsibilities required to accomplish a complete piece of work—that is, doing a job from beginning to end—within a group of manageable size. Teams put together those who need to coordinate.

Teams also reduce the number of times that work has to be transferred from one department or function to another. This reduces the opportunity for miscommunication across organizational boundaries and misunderstanding about responsibilities.

For example, a major telephone company has been developing a plan to put a team together that will enable team members to handle several functions that were handled previously by different departments. This will enable the customer to get a phone installed or repaired without being transfered to several departments.

Lawler also points out where problems might occur with work teams.

- Salary costs will go up.
- Training costs will go up.
- Additional support personnel may be needed for training.
- Unmet expectations for organizational change can occur.
- Resistance by middle management can be a problem.
- Resistance by staff support groups can occur.
- Unmet expectations for personal growth and development can occur.
- Conflict between participants and nonparticipants can be a problem if only a few teams are formed.
- Time is lost in team meetings, and decisions may be slow.[9]

---

[8] Edward E. Lawler III, *High Involvement Management* (San Francisco: Jossey-Bass, 1986), pp. 110–113.

[9] Ibid.

Many of the problems associated with teams have to do with implementing them. They are related to the problems of changing organizations—that is, the problems of changing expectations, roles, and organizational processes and systems. There are also the problems of learning how to operate effectively as a team. These problems will be addressed later in this book and methods suggested for dealing with them.

Perhaps the most difficult issue is the impact upon the established career ladders. Organizing around teams can change the types of opportunities toward which people have been working.

First, the number of levels in the organization usually is reduced, resulting in fewer "management" positions. For instance, if the supervisory level is eliminated, it becomes harder to move from being a team member to a superintendent. It may be too big a jump.

Second, growth or advancement is often by learning additional skills; therefore, movement is often lateral, rather than vertical.

In searching for solutions to these dilemmas, organizations are finding that, as employees take on more self-management and new skills, they grow far beyond past experience. As a result, they are perhaps better prepared for vertical movement than they were in the old organization. Organizations also need to find ways to make lateral movement desirable and rewarding.

To determine if organizing around teams offers an advantage for your organization will require some analysis. This involves understanding where organizational interdependencies exist and if organizing these areas into teams offers an advantage. Also, it involves understanding whether teams will help the organization to better respond to the demands being placed upon it. A process for analyzing whether teams are right for your organization will be presented in Chapter Two.

KEYS TO SUCCESS

We have learned many things over the last several years about successfully moving to a team-based organization. The keys to success are presented here, so you can see how they are incorporated into the planning and processes outlined in the book.

The conceptualization of all of our experiences into five factors came about when a colleague and I were reflecting on our day when working with a client The client was several years into a major employee involvement change effort that used employee problem-solving teams. The internal training and development staff had been telling us of the successes they were experiencing in several of their branch offices. They had over 100 such offices.

As we talked, we began to hypothesize on why some branches were more successful than others. "Success" being loosely defined as having installed problem-solving teams and having both employees and management saying they make significant contributions to the business and to employee job satisfaction.

We began to speculate why other clients were experiencing success with their team-based change efforts. We decided to find the secret to the success stories by focusing on what they felt were the keys. Over the next several months, we interviewed employees, managers, and union stewards, asking them basically what were the factors that most contributed to their successfully implementing team-based organization improvement efforts.

At first, we thought we had at least 15 key factors that contributed to success. However, the more we analyzed and discussed them the more we realized there was no magic formula nor 15 buttons to push but only five very basic principles that underlay all of the efforts. These were not new or startling discoveries. What was startling, however, was the frequency with which these basics were either overlooked, disregarded, or omitted from some of the "unsuccessful efforts."

X   The five key factors for success are:

1. The organization's goals and the change strategy—that is, teamwork—are congruent.
2. Management, union, and employee support: There is support at all levels.

3. Leadership by key people: They provide a clear vision and actively participate in the change effort.

4. A planned adaptive approach: The application of the change is flexible versus a rigid adherence to pre-established guidelines and timetables.

5. Employees and management possess the needed knowledge and skill: Everyone has the knowledge and skills necessary to perform his or her job and to work in teams.

Figure 1–1 provides a way of visualizing how the factors for success fit together.

FIGURE 1–1
Key Elements of Success

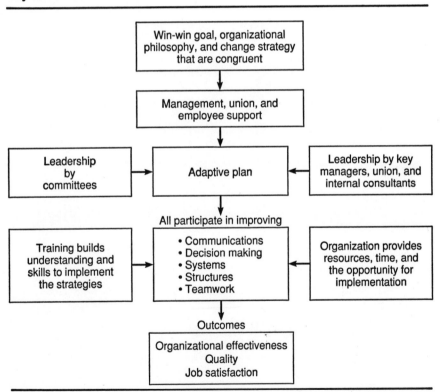

SUMMARY

Teams are a function of the coordination required to accomplish work and primarily are created to increase employee contributions and productivity. Where coordination is required, teams have made a significant contribution to organization effectiveness and employee satisfaction. Their success depends upon several key factors: a clear adaptive team plan that is congruent with the organization's goals, management and employee support and leadership, and the knowledge and skills to work in a team.

The following chapters will address these factors and the many choices managers need to make to more fully utilize teams as a way to improve organizational effectiveness.

Chapter Two

Are Teams Right for Your Organization?

A s outlined in Chapter One, team-based organizations are created for many reasons. In the early 1970s, General Foods built a team-based manufacturing facility to increase productivity, quality, flexibility to respond to changing demands, employee participation, growth and commitment, and decrease costs. There was considerable analysis of previously built company facilities and a desire to do something that was more effective and could respond to the changing marketplace demands.

In the end, most companies that are organizing around teams are doing it because they believe it will improve some part of their operation.

> The growing complexity of transacting business in response to a multitude of changes in today's environment, such as expanding governmental regulations and accelerating technology, has created a need to assemble people with the skills needed to respond to these demands into work teams.[1]

One can hardly open a magazine or read a new book on the subject of management without seeing the word *team* or reading that

---

[1] James H. Shonk, *Working in Teams* (New York: Amacom Press, 1982). Second printing by The Team Center, a division of Shonk & Associates, Ridgefield, Connecticut.

organizations are installing quality circle teams, problem-solving teams, and autonomous work teams that do the planning and decision making required to run their areas. These organizations are seeing teams as an effective response to some need.

It is quite likely, as higher levels of expertise are needed to solve more and more complex issues, that people with diverse disciplines and functions will need to come together to perform the organization's work. Teams offer an effective, proven way to manage these interdependencies.

Your organization already may consist of a number of teams. You probably have teams within and across functions and departments. The nature of the work and the extent of coordination required are the prime determinants of whether a team exists. Therefore, your first task should be to determine where teams already exist. Never mind if they are formally recognized as teams. Rather, determine where they exist and then ask how formally should the organization recognize this and what needs to be done to support better teamwork.

Perhaps all or only parts of your organization should be structured around teams. Teams are simply a way of organizing to support an interdependence that already exists and requires closer coordination between the parts. Placing the skills and responsibility for accomplishing work within a team empowers them, and it allows employees to use their talents to their fullest to accomplish the organization's goals.

TEAM ANALYSIS

Teams can be the result of an organizational analysis of productivity, morale, or turnover. Frequently, the creation of teams is the result of an analysis of what the demands are on the organization and how teams can help respond to these demands. Beckhard and Harris outline an open systems planning process, for determining those demands on the organization that might be helpful for this purpose.[2]

---

[2] Richard Beckhard and Reuben T. Harris, *Organizational Transitions: Managing Complex Change* (Reading, Mass.: Addison-Wesley Publishing, 1977), chap. 3, pp. 16–27.

Upon understanding the marketplace demands, the next step is to determine to what extent teams presently exist and how they are responding to the demands. You also should determine the extent of future teamwork that is desired to improve the organization's response.

The team Interdependence Questionnaire, which follows, is designed for these purposes. It helps to identify the extent of interdependence or teamwork that presently exists and the desired future amount of teamwork. We will address other forms of team analysis and organization readiness in Chapters Five and Seven.

Some organizations have formed teams without first determining the level of interdependence required to perform the task. The result is a group, not a team. If the task does not require coordination, a team is not needed. Such groups usually spend an inordinate amount of time early in their life trying to identify common goals and priorities. When they can't, they frequently either disband or fade away.

By defining the desired level of teamwork, you ensure that you are not just creating teams as the latest fad. You are responding to what is required to most effectively perform work.

Interdependence Questionnaire

The purpose of these questions is to determine the amount of interdependence within your organization—that is, the extent of coordination required to accomplish work.

They are intended to be used to stimulate your thinking and generate a discussion with other members of your organization about the advantages or disadvantages of increased emphasis on teamwork.

Instructions: Complete the questions by placing an *N* above the number for the statement that best describes the organization *now*, and an *F* above the statement that is more desirable for the *future*. List in the comments section some recent examples that illustrate your choice.

The higher the rating, the higher the interdependence and the greater the need for teamwork. The questions can be answered by looking across or within functions, departments, or divisions of an organization. Be sure to indicate whether you are answering the questions with a cross-functional focus or focusing within a work unit.

Analyzing the Questionnaire

Upon completing the questionnaire, all the respondents—usually 6 to 10 key managers—should discuss their results.

Interdependence Questionnaire

Do the jobs require team members to coordinate & accomplish the team task?

1. How are goals accomplished?

1	2	3
By individual effort.	By two or more functions coordinating their efforts.	By several functions coordinating their efforts.

Comments: _____

_____

2. How are resources allocated?

1	2	3
Functions have their own separate resources.	Functions share some common resources.	Large parts of the organization share and allocate common resources.

Comments: _____

_____

3. How is work accomplished?

1	2	3
By working alone.	By some functions coordinating their activities.	By all functions coordinating their activities.

Comments: _____

_____

A. Identify major pieces of work that require coordination with others.

_____

_____

Comments· _____

_____

4. How is planning done?

1	2	3
Planning and progress feedback is done individually.	Planning and progress feedback is done in subgroups.	Planning and progress feedback is done by a collection of functions/ departments.

Comments: _____

_____

5. How are we communicating?

1	2	3
Communications are primarily within functions.	Some cross-functional communication is needed.	Frequent cross-functional communications are needed.

Comments: _____

_____

6. What type of meetings are held?

1	2	3
Meetings are mostly held within a function.	Some meetings are cross-functional.	Frequent cross-functional or total organization meetings are needed.

Comments: _____

_____

7. How are decisions made?

1	2	3
Decisions are made individually and do not impact the work of others.	Decisions are made by two or more people and impact the work of others.	Decisions are made by consensus of several functions and impact the work of most.

Comments: _____

_____

8. What is the time frame for coordination across functions?

1	2	3
Functions work for months before coordination is needed.	Coordination is needed weekly.	Activities must be coordinated on a daily basis.

Comments: _____

_____

Each person should explain his or her answers for each item and discuss them for understanding. Avoid merely obtaining a numerical average for each question. Rather, strive for an understanding of everyone's point of view.

A consensus should be reached about the desired future level of interdependence. Circle the response that best represents the consensus on how the organization should function in the future.

The higher the number on each scale, the higher the need for teamwork. If responses are always at the left end of each scale, there is a low need for teamwork and the organization should be less concerned about trying to organize around teams.

If there is little interdependence, employees will see little or no value in functioning more effectively together. The farther to the right responses are, the more value employees will see in operating as a team.

High scores on desired future interdependence will indicate the need to create more teamwork. Low scores obviously mean that more teams are not the answer

DETERMINING THE ADVANTAGES OF TEAMS

After determining the present and desired future level of interdependence, discuss the following questions to help determine if organizing around teams or improving teamwork will offer an advantage to your organization.

Is the interdependence of employees high or low?

A. Within functions, departments, and the like.
B. Across functions or departments

How and where would better coordination and teamwork improve the organization's ability to address marketplace demands—for example, improve productivity, quality, customer service?

How and where would empowering teams of employees to perform their work benefit the organization and employees?

For example, a credit-oriented customer service organization is using teams of employees composed of several functions. They are finding that they can respond to customer questions more fully with less delay and that employees have a greater understanding of all operations and, therefore, feel more confident in answering customer questions.

How does having employee teams fit with the long-term goals and business strategy of the organization?

The long-term goal of research for one organization is to improve the transition of ideas from research to production to marketing. The firm has developed teams consisting of these functions to accomplish that goal.

What influence will employee teams have on employee job satisfaction and commitment to the organization?

A manufacturing organization felt that employee commitment and job satisfaction and quality could be increased if employees were involved in solving problems they encountered while making the product. They formed problem-solving teams, and their successes have led them to include teams in decision making and planning how work is accomplished.

What impact will moving toward a team-based organization have upon the resources required?

Short term—many organizations require increased resources for training. *Long term*—many experience a reduction in management and staff personnel required as the team assumes its responsibilities.

After discussing the results of the Interdependence Questionnaire and each person's response to the advantages of teams, you should have an idea of whether teams will help your organization—and where. Don't be concerned if you can't answer the questions about how to organize teams. That information comes later. However, you should be aware of some circumstances early in the planning process that make organizing around teams difficult or perhaps improbable.

ISSUES THAT MAKE ORGANIZING AROUND TEAMS DIFFICULT

Low Interdependence

If, in fact, employees do not need to coordinate and can perform their jobs independently, they do not need to be a team. Sales organizations frequently fall into this category.

If salespeople have a private territory and their own resources, they are for the most part independent. If they share a territory or resources or help one another during special promotions, they are somewhat interdependent.

Geographic Separation

Physical separation makes it difficult for teams to meet, plan, communicate, and make decisions—and for members to help each other.

Size

Sometimes the number of people who are interdependent is so large that planning and decision making become very difficult. The correct size can vary considerably, depending on the complexity of the task and the maturity of the team members. Large teams of 15 or more people may find it difficult to reach team decisions.

SUMMARY

There is no magic formula for deciding when and where to create teams. However, an analysis of the interdependence required to perform work and of how teams might improve organizational effectiveness will help make this determination. Hopefully, the previous questions and the following chapters will help you decide what is best for your organization.

Chapter Three
Types of Teams

P rovided that you have decided teams can help your organization, the next question you face is what types of teams are
needed. I am not speaking of whether the teams should be temporary, cross-functional, or a diagonal slice. These are all important decisions, which will have to be made based on the problem
or nature of work and the resources required to perform it.

Rather, I am speaking of what I believe to be a more fundamental question that often is overlooked. The question is how much
autonomy the teams should have. The reason this is an extremely
important question is because the greater the amount of autonomy given a team the more likely it will affect the organization's
structure and processes. Furthermore, the amount of autonomy
given a team can greatly affect productivity, flexibility, costs, and
management effort to sustain teams.

These items are all connected, and it is difficult if not impossible to change one without affecting the others. As the manager of
the team, you will need to understand how these variables interact and how the amount of team autonomy can affect them.

To examine these issues further, let's first look at what others
say about teams and participation.

TEAMS AND PARTICIPATION

In addition to teams being a way to respond to increased demand for coordination and productivity, they also can be designed to meet employees' needs for increased self-control and participation in the workplace.

Walton talks about teams and the ways they function as the key ingredients in moving from a control strategy—where employees are controlled by external forces, such as management—to a commitment strategy—where employees are committed to the organization and exercise more self-control.[1]

Key elements of Walton's commitment strategy that fit closely with a team-based organization are:

- Jobs that emphasize a whole task—that is, doing a job from beginning to end—and combine doing with thinking.
- Flexible duties contingent on changing conditions.
- A flat organization structure—that is, few levels, with mutual influence by both management and employees.
- Minimum status differentials to deemphasize hierarchy.
- Coordination and control, based on shared goals, values, and traditions.
- Variable rewards to create equity and to reinforce group achievements—for example, gain-sharing and profit-sharing, and pay linked to skill mastery.
- Employment security.
- Employee participation is encouraged on a wide range of issues.
- Business data are shared widely.[2]

At the center of Walton's theories is the belief that enlisting employee commitment through participation will lead to enhanced performance.

---

[1] Richard E. Walton, "From Control to Commitment in the Workplace," *Harvard Business Review*, March/April 1985, pp. 77–84.

[2] Ibid.

McGregor's Theory Y was one of the pioneer efforts to point organizations in the direction of an understanding that meeting employees' needs can facilitate meeting the organization's goals.[3] Trist and other socio-technical theorists advocate joining the social system (employees' needs) with the technical system (the organization's technology) to optimize an organization's effectiveness.[4]

Sashkin speaks of three basics that human beings need from their work. They need autonomy and control over the workplace, task achievement, and co-worker relations. He says that by participating in goal setting, problem solving, decision making, and planning change, employees experience autonomy and meaningfulness in their work. This leads to commitment to the organization, innovation, improved performance, and organizational productivity. These needs can be met through participation in an effectively designed work team.

Sashkin also states that, when properly designed and implemented, the participative management of work will result in performance and productivity improvements, and it will satisfy the three basic human work needs.[5] Failure to satisfy these needs is harmful to employees. Therefore, he concludes that participative management is an ethical imperative.

Lawler states:

> [T]eams can be the basic building block upon which a high-involvement organization is constructed. They have the potential to be highly effective if they fit the technology and the rest of the organization is designed to support them.[6]

These writers are saying that increased organizational effectiveness is closely linked with employee participation and with their needs being met in the context of accomplishing the organiza-

[3] Douglas McGregor, *The Human Side of Enterprise* (McGraw-Hill, 1960).

[4] E. L. Trist and K. W. Bamforth, "Some Social Psychological Consequences of the Long Wall Method of Coal-Getting," *Human Relations* 1951, 4, pp. 3–38.

[5] Marshall Sashkin, "Participative Management Is an Ethical Imperative," *Organizational Dynamics*, American Management Association, Spring 1984, pp. 5–22.

[6] Edward E. Lawler III, *High Involvement Management* (San Francisco: Jossey-Bass, 1986).

tion's mission. Accomplishing organizational goals, employee participation, and meeting employees' needs are synergistic and consistent with participative work teams.

For some organizations, highly participative teams are a reality and for others perhaps a target to aim for. My experience to date with teams within client organizations has shown that high levels of employee participation and teamwork are very complimentary. However, every organization has its unique character and will have in use various levels of employee participation.

Organizations must start where they are and determine the appropriate level of employee participation and teamwork, given their unique character and needs. Just as creating teams should be the result of an analysis of needs, so should the level of participation be the result of organizational and employee needs.

Frequently, employees and managers tend to engage in what I call 0 to 100 percent thinking. If they are at 0 relative to the use of participation, they think in terms of jumping immediately to 100 percent. Such a jump is hard to make, because managers and employees frequently do not possess the skills required and frequently lack understanding of how to make such a change. Furthermore, it may not be the appropriate response for an organization's needs. Therefore, it frequently is best to start slow and deliberately plan the magnitude of the change and the time required.

TEAM AUTONOMY

The amount of autonomy given to a team can range from making suggestions, to problem solving, to self-management. The greater the autonomy, the higher the potential for employees to contribute to their maximum. Obviously, the nature of the work—such as its complexity, the amount of training needed, and the teams' potential impact on other parts of the organization—are all factors that determine how much autonomy a team can assume and how fast. The following diagram (Figure 3–1) illustrates how team autonomy can differ by type of team.[7]

---

[7] Edward E. Lawler, III, and Susan A. Mohrman, "Quality of Work Life," unpublished manuscript, 1984. Original chart adapted.

FIGURE 3–1
Team Autonomy

Low _____ High

Suggestion Teams	Problem-solving Teams	Semiautonomous Teams	Self-managing Teams
Advisory committees	Quality circles	Business unit teams	Business unit teams
Suggestion teams	Interfunctional teams	Work unit teams	Autonomous work teams
	Total system task forces		

Teams at the left of the team autonomy scale represent a fairly low level of autonomy, with no decision making. They frequently require little or no change in the level of employee participation or in the organization structure and work processes.

The second column is typical of teams that focus primarily on problem solving and can be maintained with relatively few changes in organization structure, participation, and processes.

Teams in the two right-hand columns usually require major changes in these variables.

Suggestion Teams

Suggestion teams are frequently temporary and exist to work on a given issue. Some organizations have permanent suggestion systems; however, they are typically individual, rather than team oriented. Suggestion team recommendations have to be approved, and the team typically has little decision-making or implementation authority. Therefore, the organization operates with the established hierarchy making decisions and implementing them. Suggestion teams can be quite helpful when a large number of ideas are desired—for example, to cut costs or increase productivity.

Problem-Solving Teams

These teams are involved in identifying and researching activities and in developing effective solutions to work-related problems. The majority of problem-solving teams consist of the supervisor and five to eight employees with common work-related concerns who identify and solve problems. Staff services or special resource persons—for example, engineers—who interact with the work group may be invited to occasionally participate or to become permanent members.

Many of the task forces are put together to recommend what the company should do on a given topic. These groups can be classified as problem-solving teams. Quality circles are another example of problem-solving teams.

Semiautonomous Teams

Semiautonomous teams are managed by a supervisor and have considerable input into the planning, organizing, and controlling of their daily work. This includes:

- Helping to establish the work unit's goals.
- Providing input into team plans.
- Identifying and recommending solutions to problems.
- Having considerable input into or making daily operating decisions.

Semiautonomous teams are used when the tasks can be best accomplished if employees have considerable freedom to act. A telephone credit service uses semiautonomous teams, giving customer-contact people considerable decision-making freedom to best handle each account. This is needed because of the wide diversity and individual differences of accounts. However, they have maintained a supervisor, who helps to coordinate across several customer service groups that are interdependent when work loads are high in one area and teams need to help each other.

Self-Managing Teams

Such teams are responsible for managing their work on a daily basis. This includes:

- Team goal setting, based upon organization goals, or having considerable input to team goals.
- Planning how goals will be accomplished.
- Allocating resources to accomplish goals.
- Identifying and solving problems within the work area.
- Making daily operating decisions within their defined level of authority.
- Recommending solutions to external problems—that is, problems caused by factors or influences outside the team's control and affecting the team's performance.
- Work scheduling.
- Hiring team members.

Self-managing teams also are used where employees need freedom to act and where the coordination needs with other teams is either low or of such degree that the team can manage it.

Manufacturing areas where teams control many of the inputs and operations that transform raw materials into a product have used autonomous teams, as have many white-collar operations.

Organizations that decide to increase team autonomy typically do it gradually. Some organizations have followed a progression from low to high team autonomy over a period of years.

Organizations having had a successful team problem-solving approach find that managers and employees have learned to work more collaboratively in problem-solving team meetings, and that these skills frequently carry over to their daily interactions. Problem-solving teams can be the practice fields for the development of skills that are needed to create a more autonomous team.

Many of the skills needed by self-managing teams, such as interpersonal communications and team problem solving, are natural outgrowths of effectively functioning problem-solving teams. Surveys with Ford and GTE also have found that employees' attitudes toward supervisors and the company have improved where the employees are involved in such teams.

Ford Motor Company and the UAW and GTE and the CWA started their employee involvement efforts several years ago with problem-solving teams. In some of their facilities they are now exploring and moving toward more self-managing work teams, which are organized around a task or service and given considerable freedom to plan and execute how the task is performed. Their early experiences with problem-solving teams have been helpful in building the skills needed to move toward more autonomous work teams.

The Team Progression diagram shown in Figure 3–2 depicts the progress of teams from problem solving, to work unit, to self-managing. In organizations like Ford—that have had employee involvement problem-solving teams where there has been a gradual evolution toward greater team autonomy—changes in roles, in organization structure, and in systems also have had to be made. Making progress—given the large number of changes—takes time, whereas newly designed organizations, like the General Foods's Topeka facility, can be designed for high team autonomy from the beginning.

FIGURE 3–2
Team Progression

Low Autonomy ———————————————————— **High Autonomy**

Problem-solving team	Semiautonomous Team	Self-managing Team
Teams reach subject or technical limitations. Either new problem-solving teams are formed or they progress to ongoing work unit teams.	Teams plan, problem-solve, and have input to goals and decisions. Requires changes in: philosophy, structure, systems, policies, and skills.	Teams run the daily business of the unit.

WHY INCREASE TEAM AUTONOMY?

Organizations that started installing suggestion and problem-solving teams and quality circles in the late 70s and 80s are beginning to move toward a higher level of team autonomy. As a result, they have experienced increases in productivity through self-managing work teams and have received requests from employees for increased involvement.

A recent study by Cohen and Ledford of self-managing work teams—SMTs—found that SMTs with supervisors tended to be less effective than those without them.[8] They did not speak in terms of team autonomy; however, one could speculate that teams without supervisors would tend to have significant autonomy.

Given the external marketplace pressures to adapt quickly to remain competitive and given the desire of employees for increased involvement, the movement to a higher level of team autonomy seems to be a natural progression. Furthermore, much of the groundwork and training needed to move toward a higher level of team autonomy already has been done by organizations that have trained managers and problem-solving teams. Without some movement toward greater autonomy and changes in processes, organizations may experience the following lost opportunities.

1. A diminishing return in organizational effectiveness. This usually is due to limits being placed on what teams can do.

2. An inability to implement more innovative and radical team ideas, because the present structure is either not supportive of them or is threatened.

For example, a problem-solving team wanted to be able to locate the lift truck in a supply yard, so the team could access it easier and facilitate movement of stock into and out of the yard. The team recommended attaching a bicycle flag, which is a flag attached to a long antenna, to the truck, so it could be spotted

[8] Susan Cohen and Gerald Ledford, Jr., "The Effectiveness of Self-Managing Teams: A Quasi-Experiment," Center for Effective Organizations, publication T91-7 (192), Graduate School of Business Administration, University of Southern California, Los Angeles, March 1991, p. 21.

over the top of the tall stacks of supplies in the yard. The team was told that the members could not do this because it was against company policy to attach nonstandard objects to company equipment. This is only one small example of how management philosophy and existing policies may not be supportive of the changes being recommended.

However, while visiting another organization that had created autonomous teams, I asked who had to approve the new ideas the teams wanted to try. The employee looked at me as if he didn't understand the question but replied, "When we come up with a new idea to improve how we work, we try it out. If it works, we keep it. If it doesn't work, we keep thinking of other ways to improve."

Obviously, in this organization there are limits to what teams can do. However the whole atmosphere is different. It is a supportive atmosphere that encourages initiative, rather than a control atmosphere to approve all new ideas.

3. Unmet expectations by employees who want greater autonomy, because they can see the benefits to them and the organization. This can lead to disillusionment and dropout in the current problem-solving effort.

For example, though many organizations are quite happy with their quality efforts, I constantly receive calls from managers who want to know how to revitalize what they perceive to be a lackluster quality circle effort. They say employees are no longer participating in teams as they had in the past, and that managers feel they are spending large amounts of time for little return. Upon further questioning of those who are disappointed in their quality circle efforts, I usually find the following:

- Quality circles come together for a specific problem and disband, instead of being ongoing work teams.
- They are low in autonomy—that is, suggestion or problem-solving groups have little or no ability to implement ideas without management approval and involvement.
- Many of the old management practices and processes are still in existence and sometimes restrict or slow down implemen-

tation of the more radical ideas that would change the existing structure or processes.

4. Complacency on the part of management. "We are okay as is. If it isn't broke, don't fix it."

SUMMARY

Increasing team autonomy is an expected progression if you want to fully utilize employee contributions. Teams gradually will be taking over the tasks performed by management, and service, and functional groups. Teams will be making decisions and implementing them in ways that may fall outside of the normal processes and hierarchical channels of control.

As teams become more autonomous, the organization will experience greater pressure to change its structures and processes. Chapter Four will explore in more detail the types of organizational changes needed to support teams.

Chapter Four

Organizational Support for Teams

T he change efforts of the 1980s concentrated on problem-solving teams, such as quality of work life, quality circles, and employee involvement. Organizations that incorporated these changes are maturing and extending the use of teams beyond problem-solving to managing their own work areas. In doing so, these organizations are realizing that this increased team autonomy requires changes in organizational structure and in systems to make them supportive of teams.

TEAM FOUNDATION

Figure 4–1, Team Foundation, illustrates the organizational structures and processes that need to support the effective operation of teams. The top box represents typical organizational goals. The next box indicates that teams are used to accomplish the goals. The items in the bottom boxes should be supportive of teams and compatible with one another.

For example, advocating decision making by the team does not fit with an organization that restricts the information and knowledge

FIGURE 4–1
Teamwork Foundation

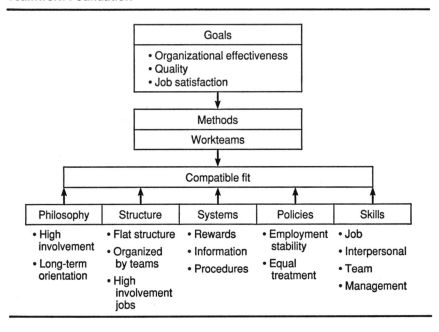

necessary to make informed, effective decisions. Furthermore, changing one aspect of how an organization functions frequently requires changes in other areas.

Increasing the team's involvement in planning requires getting more information to the team. It also may cause staff, such as planners and the like, to work more closely with the teams. Increasing teamwork requires examining the items in the bottom boxes to make sure they are supportive of teamwork as well as compatible with each other.

Many organizations that started quality circles and employee involvement teams may have difficulty sustaining their efforts. In order to move to a higher level of team autonomy, the organizations must consciously decide what changes are indicated after reviewing the team foundation.

Such areas as philosophy, structure, systems, policies, and skills are possible targets for changes. Your organization may not be ready for nor require significant changes to improve its use of teams. Your plan should determine what changes are needed to match the degree of team autonomy desired.

Typically, increasing team autonomy involves reducing the number of levels in the organization and changing the role of management. This can be threatening to employees and may be resisted by those who fear what impact the change will have on their future. Therefore, a clear vision of where the organization is heading and how roles will change can help employees making this transition. How roles change will be addressed in Chapter Nine.

ORGANIZATION PHILOSOPHY

High Involvement

The organization's philosophy of management and core values must be supportive of work teams. The core values and philosophies of organizations using work teams frequently emphasize beliefs in involving people and placing high trust in them.

Lawler has identified three basic assumptions about people that represent high involvement philosophies, which are necessary for a participative team-based organization.

- People can be trusted to make important decisions about their work activities.
- People can develop the knowledge to make important decisions about the management of their work activities.
- When people make decisions about the management of their work, the result is greater organizational effectiveness.[1]

An underlying theme in these statements is trust in the ability and intent of employees.

Management behaviors must be consistent with this philosophy. Otherwise, employees will receive a dual message, and the

---

[1] Edward E. Lawler III, *High Involvement Management* (San Francisco: Jossey-Bass, 1986), p. 193.

effort to give employees more opportunity to participate on work teams will lose credibility.

In one organization, after the manager explained the management philosophy and stressed the need for trust, an employee asked, "How long will this approach last?" The manager's response was, "We will never stop trusting you."

The following is an example of a Fortune 500 client's mission and philosophy that is supportive of work teams.

Mission Statement
Mission

Our mission is to competitively provide quality products and services that satisfy customer needs and expectations.

Philosophy

To accomplish our mission we must meet the needs of the individual and the business by creating an environment where employees take pride in their work, and derive enjoyment from the workplace and satisfaction from accomplishing the company mission. Our philosophy will be based upon:

Trust and Respect.   An open and trusting climate is necessary to maintain a motivating and rewarding work environment. Open and honest communications, fair treatment, and equitable practices will be the foundation of our operations.

Teamwork.   We are most effective when we work together as a team. Teamwork requires flexibility, sharing information, and creating opportunities to contribute ideas and participate in decision making.

Involvement.   People support what they help to create. Involvement in the business, through teamwork, and communication of business plans and customer expectations, results in understanding, ownership, and commitment.

Continuous Improvement.   We must continually strive for excellence in what we do. Creativity, innovation, and risk taking will be encouraged. Continuous improvement will enhance our ability to remain competitive.

Growth and Development.   Professional growth and skill development provides the individual with a sense of accomplishment and enables continued contributions toward the improvement of the business.

Long-Term Orientation

A long-term orientation for business plans and people management is common among team-based organizations. This frequently is exemplified by investment in equipment, training, career development, and labor stability.

Some organizations have developed mission statements that reinforce their long-term commitment and define how they treat employees. For example, Ford Motor Credit's mission statement emphasizes the importance of meeting employee needs and teamwork as an important part of accomplishing organizational goals.

Ford Credit's Commitment Statement

Our mission at Ford Credit is to offer a broad range of financial services recognized as the best. We are committed to excellence in all that we do. Established values and guiding principles form the foundation for our efforts to achieve this goal. As our reputation for excellence increases, so, too, will our profitability and growth.

The key to accomplishing this mission is serving our customers. Because customer satisfaction results from the efforts of our people, we place a high value on their expertise, pride, and dedication. We strive always:

- To create an atmosphere of trust and respect among our employees and our customers.
- To encourage self-improvement and career development through training in job and communication skills.
- To support innovation and ingenuity.
- To promote teamwork and sharing of ideas through employee involvement at all levels.
- To encourage and reward individual achievements and contributions.
- To support our people with ongoing improvements in technology and facilities.

(Reprinted with permission of Ford Motor Credit.)

The management philosophy is a prelude to the development of win/win goals. The goals of a team-based organization must be "win/win," meaning they will benefit all parties. If they are to give long-term support, management, union, and employees must all see there is something to be gained. Flowery statements that speak only about benefits to one segment will not be trusted or believed.

Increased effectiveness, involvement, and consideration of the individual should be the basis for formulating goals. Considering and involving employees as the organization strives for increased effectiveness, is a win/win approach.

ORGANIZATIONAL STRUCTURE

Flat Structure

Many newly designed team-based organizations are challenging the traditional hierarchical structure by reducing the number of levels and staff support. Decision-making responsibility, frequently handled by supervisors or staff groups, is delegated to the work team.

A lean, flat organization structure is compatible with higher levels of involvement and the movement of responsibility to lower levels. Adding levels tends to add reviews and raises the level of decision making. The trend in high involvement team-based organizations is toward fewer levels and less staff.

The staff operates primarily in a training and consulting capacity. The work previously done by staff groups is performed by work teams. For example, some work teams handle their own hiring, raw material ordering, production scheduling, and training.

Organized by Teams

Organizations concerned with customer service are finding that teams of employees, who are trained to handle several functions, provide better and more efficient customer service than purely functional organizations.

To illustrate, a major telephone company is planning for a team to handle dispatch, assignment, repair, and testing, which were separate functions. When a customer calls, any member of the team can handle all four functions, thereby reducing the number of times a customer gets transferred because someone says, "That's not my job."

A strong functional orientation to accomplishing work often works against teamwork. For example, goals are set, reviewed, and rewarded by function. Therefore, that is where people put their attention.

Getting the product or service to market and providing good customer service, however, requires cross-functional teamwork. Because goals are set separately, people may not recognize that they are part of a team. They see their contribution as one of several individual acts that hopefully add up to a well-delivered finished product.

If the tasks are very discreet and simple, a functional focus can be very efficient. However, as the tasks begin to flow into one another, overlap, and become complex, more cooperation or teamwork is required. The research function of one major corporation is finding it easier to get products manufactured and marketed if members of those functions are on the team that plans and guides the product's development from research to manufacturing.

Separating work by function and identifying discreet tasks will limit the information flow, the employee's ability to see the big picture, and their control of and, therefore, commitment to the overall task. It also will cut down on employee interaction, which can have a negative impact on productivity and job satisfaction.

To overcome these problems, a major manufacturer has made the repair of its machinery the responsibility of both the maintenance and production functions. The past practice was to let maintenance fix the machine while production took a break. As a result, little information was exchanged between the operator and maintenance person, and both saw the other as responsible for the machine's productivity.

Now they work together during short-term and preventive

maintenance efforts and have been able to show significant enough gains in machine productivity to justify additional maintenance resources. It also has reduced the "that's not my job" feeling on the part of both parties and the finger pointing when problems arise.

There are advantages, of course, to a strong functional organization:

1. It promotes an in-depth knowledge or focus on a given discipline or body of knowledge. People can become experts in one area.

2. Employees can be more efficiently trained when they are trained to perform work in one area.

The disadvantages of a functional organization are:

1. It is often more difficult to communicate across functional lines. Special meetings have to be called or, sometimes, people not among one's daily contacts have to be notified.

2. Employees only have a part of the picture. A typical illustration is, "I don't know if marketing can help you with the problem—I only work in sales."

3. Employees are focused on a specific job, versus the overall mission of the team. A specific illustration is, "My job is to run the cash register, yours is to bag the groceries. Who cares if the customer has to wait?"

4. All of the above make it especially difficult for employees to give good customer service.

The advantages of a team-based organization are:

1. Multi-functional teams reduce the number of handoffs and the amount of coordination required across functions. Because more of the expertise to do the job is on the team, there is less need to pass work to other areas.

2. Teams can be more self-regulatory and self-contained, thereby reducing the need for external controls. The skills needed to perform a complete piece of work are usually on the team. Team members are involved in setting goals for their area and, therefore, usually are committed to them.

If teams are given adequate feedback about their performance, all the ingredients exist for greater self-control.

3. Employees are focused on the team's mission, versus a specific job. They see the "big picture."

After working on a team, an employee said to me, "In my old job I thought issues were simple, and I couldn't understand why management either couldn't decide or made the wrong decision. Now that I am involved and get the same information that management gets, I understand the big picture and realize many of the decisions are not simple. In fact, I find myself agreeing with management on most issues."

The disadvantages of a team-based organization are:

1. More training with a broader scope is required. Employees will need to be trained to do more tasks, so they can rotate and fill in for each other and provide a broader range of customer services.

2. Some of the in-depth focus could be lessened. Asking employees to perform a broader range of tasks could put less emphasis on being a specialist and the development of high expertise in one area.

3. Some decisions may be slower, especially now that more people—that is, team members—may be included in the decision. Short-term daily operating decisions frequently are made by individuals on the job. Long-term policy decisions or decisions about work allocation or who gets what training frequently are made by the team.

High Involvement Jobs

In high involvement organizations, work teams are responsible for a large variety of tasks. The team is responsible for measuring and evaluating its own work, which incorporates performance feedback and a sense of responsibility for results. Teams assume responsibility for many of their own personnel functions, such as training and hiring.

Individuals gradually become proficient in this wide variety of tasks and functions. This proficiency makes it possible for the team to flexibly assign tasks, and for the individual to rotate among a range of responsibilities.[2]

SYSTEMS

Rewards

Many of the changes toward higher participation and teamwork, such as increased communications, working in a more collaborative mode, and increasing employee participation in decision making, require changes in employees' and managers' behavior. For these changes to occur and continue, they must be encouraged and rewarded.

The reward systems most commonly associated with high involvement organizations are gain-sharing, profit-sharing, employee ownership, skill-based pay, an all-salary work force, and flexible benefits. In the first three, employees share in the cost savings, the profits, and the organizational growth. Skill-based systems pay employees for the number of tasks they can perform. Such systems encourage and support job rotation and learning new skills.

To reinforce the behaviors associated with high involvement teams, Lawler says the organization's reward system must support the core values of organizational commitment, self-management, personal and career growth, and flexibility.[3]

The many ways in which people are presently rewarded, either psychologically or monetarily, must be examined to determine whether they are supportive of the changes desired. For example, the goal-setting and performance evaluation systems of most organizations are designed for individuals or functions. They should be examined to determine what changes are needed to support teams.

Within most organizations, career paths provide vertical growth. Team-based organizations tend to have flatter structures.

---

[2] Ibid., chap. 7, pp. 101–18.
[3] Ibid., p. 202.

They emphasize people acquiring multiple skills, and they foster career paths that are lateral and that broaden people's knowledge, versus increasing or creating more in-depth or specialized experience.

Managers must be rewarded for developing people. To illustrate, picture an announcement of a new vice presidential appointment saying a prime reason for the promotion was that he or she developed people.

Occasionally, when I speak to groups of managers about teams and teamwork, I will be asked this question: "Why do you need teams if managers are doing a good job?" Further questioning of what is meant usually reveals the following: The manager believes that his or her job is to manage a department and that, when the manager needs to coordinate with other departments, he or she will.

With this vision of a manager's responsibilities, it is understandable that his or her first priority is managing the department, and, perhaps, that is as it should be in some organizations. However, I frequently see this priority overriding attention to cross-departmental coordination. I frequently talk to top executives who say one of their biggest challenges is to get various parts of the organization to work together.

During a training seminar with the top management of one major corporation, a manager coined the phrase "functional nationalism." By this he was referring to the tendency in this organization for managers to manage within their function and to give cross-functional integration of work little or no attention. He said that managers worked as if they were managing within a long cylindrical tube. They manage up and down the tubes but not across. On making these statements, he received considerable support from his colleagues.

Shortly after the seminar, this organization began to set joint goals. All functions would meet together and set joint company-wide goals that legitimized their interdependence and rewarded cross-functional coordination. In addition to organizing by teams, the organization's reward system and processes need to support teamwork.

Information

Clearly, for teams to make more and better decisions and to self-manage their activities, they need sufficient information. The advent of the personal computer certainly makes it easier to get more information to more people in less time than before.

In one organization, a large illuminated bulletin board flashes the daily news to all employees, and a repeating message on a video screen in the corporate office vestibule gives the latest information about the corporation. Another uses cards on tables and banners on luncheon walls to relay current messages. In many companies, employees and the union attend meetings previously only the province of management.

The old attitude of screening information to determine what is "privileged" will need to give way to searching for the information needed to help employees do their job. Team-based organizations must strive for systematic, effective, but not burdensome, methods of sharing information.

Procedures

Daily operating procedures usually can be altered to provide more involvement of employees. Planned changes in daily operating procedures provide an ideal time for employees to become involved in their development, rather than waiting until after the change has taken place. Examples of daily operating procedures or changes that might benefit from greater involvement of affected employees are:

- Involving employees in determining the shift rotation schedule.
- Consulting office staff before changing computer systems and software.
- Consulting equipment operators before repairs or changes are made.
- Consulting those who produce a product before making engineering changes to improve quality.

- Involving employees in selecting candidates for a new maintenance apprentice program.

When planning team responsibilities, existing procedures should be reviewed to determine how they should involve teams to improve:

- Organization effectiveness.
- Product quality.
- Job satisfaction.

POLICIES

Employment Stability

Essential to asking employees to improve operations and cut costs is the assurance that doing so will not cost them their jobs. Employment stability tied to loss of market share cannot always be controlled.

However, team-based organizations like General Foods's Topeka plant have found ways to minimize the impact of temporary downturns on sales by utilizing employees in equipment maintenance during slow periods.

Profit-sharing, which allows a fluctuation up or down of total compensation and a lean structure that keeps overhead low, also can help during hard times.

The 1982 agreement between Ford Motor Company and the UAW contained such elements as a guaranteed income stream and profit-sharing designed expressly to address job and income security. It also created the Mutual Growth Forum.

"It was designed to promote sound management union relations through better communications, systematic fact-finding, and advance discussion of business developments that are of material interest to the union, employees and the company."[4] The

---

[4] Ernest J. Savoie and Donald F. Ephlin, "The New Ford–UAW Agreement: Its Work-life Aspects," *The Work Life Review*, Michigan Quality of Work Life Council, vol. 1, issue 1, pp. 3–7.

forum provides a vehicle for preventive problem-solving on job security.

Equal Treatment

The feeling of equality is essential to feeling part of the team. Many organizations have reduced or eliminated the status differences between management and employees that can cause a separation and "we/they" feeling. In these organizations, management still is seen as having more decision-making authority and as providing direction.

However, the managers also are viewed as readily accessible and part of the team. Policies and practices that treat people equally, coupled with the other building blocks previously mentioned, can go a long way in building teamwork.

In one organization that was engaged in an employee involvement effort, the chief counsel of its legal department was approached by the secretaries to tell him they felt that the policy restricting secretaries but not managers from taking vacations around major holidays was not treating them as equal to management. He agreed and asked who created the policy and was informed that he had. He immediately rescinded the policy.

The following are examples of ways in which organizations have attempted to treat all employees as members of the team:

- No reserved parking spaces.
- Everyone has access to the same facilities—cafeteria, meeting rooms, and the like.
- Rules, policies, and procedures are the same for everyone and are written by employee/management committees.
- There are few symbols of status differences in offices and dress.
- Employees are represented on committees that typically are solely the province of management.
- Employees review management's performance and vice versa.

SKILLS

Involving people without ensuring that they have the proper training and skills to perform their newly acquired tasks is a quick route to many mistakes—and to the reinforcement of the doubters who said it wouldn't work.

The four most commonly needed skills are:

Job—typing, welding, computer operation, assembly.

Interpersonal—listening, communicating, conflict resolution, giving and receiving feedback.

Team—team planning, problem solving, decision making, meetings.

Management—planning, leading, coaching.

It is essential that organizations provide time and resources for employees to develop these skills. Frequently, the short-term perspective dominates, and organizations are reluctant to invest in training. The result is usually a perpetuation of the status quo, because employees and managers do not develop the skills needed to operate differently. The type of training needed to launch a team-based organization will be discussed in Chapter Eight.

SUMMARY

Increased teamwork and team autonomy can be an effective strategy for increasing organizational effectiveness and employee satisfaction. However, for a team-based strategy to prosper, organizations must examine their philosophy, structures, systems, policies, and skills to ensure that they are compatible with the amount of team autonomy desired—and are compatible with each other.

Many new organization start-ups have been effective, because they have this type of total systems approach to organization change. In an existing organization, immediately changing all of these is improbable and not recommended. It is usually a gradual evolution over time.

Chapter Five
Getting Started

W hile working on an employee involvement (EI) effort with a major corporation, one of the company's internal change agents asked if most efforts took as long as theirs had to get started. Several months had been taken to build support among key managers and the union and to overcome their concerns. And several obstacles had been encountered during the first three months, including lack of support from the international union. The change agent said that an installation of "quality circles" at another location had only taken a matter of weeks.

However, approximately two months later, that effort came to a sudden halt, due to the many concerns expressed by both union and management and the failure to set expectations and gain agreement about the nature and magnitude of the change effort.

News of failed or fizzled change efforts is constant. Frequently, these failures are related directly to the amount and quality of prework and planning done, and the extent to which the effort is seen as a serious commitment to a major change in the functioning of the organization.

Many organizations are anxious to start teams immediately. Consequently, planning either is overlooked or done hurriedly. Clearly, though, it is during the planning and startup phase that assumptions and decisions are made that will affect the ultimate direction.

One organization was so eager to start employee problem-solving teams that it sent a letter to all employees asking for volunteers. The company did not consider how to put the teams of volunteers together, so it randomly assembled the volunteers into teams. After several months, managers were disappointed, because the teams were working on such subjects as the food in the cafeteria, parking lot issues, and vending machines.

A closer look at why teams were not taking on work-flow issues revealed that, by randomly putting together teams, the company had not put together teams of people who were interdependent—that is, who had to work together to accomplish their tasks. Therefore, the only things members shared were environmental issues that everybody in the facility had in common. Some preliminary goal setting and analysis of what kinds of teams were needed to accomplish the goals may have eliminated this false start.

The Readiness Planning Questionnaire presented later in this chapter is designed to raise the issues an organization should address when undertaking a team-based change effort. The questionnaire helps to identify some of the areas on which to focus during the early planning phase. Initial plans must be continually updated as a myriad of issues arise that, at the beginning, cannot be predicted.

A team-based approach to increasing organizational effectiveness sets into motion many complex organizational and personal changes that have to be considered while planning the change. Such an approach changes the roles traditionally assumed by management, union, and employees. It requires a different union stance and different employee attitudes toward the company and their work. These attitudes do not change so much by talking about them but come from the experience of working together in a different, more collaborative way.

In one unionized organization, a union steward at first was very skeptical of the organization's employee involvement (EI) efforts and how they might change his role. After a year's experience with the effort, he was telling stewards from other company locations that he had much more influence in planning what was done and had to react less frequently to "poor management decisions." He informed them that they were missing an opportunity to do what is best for the employees if they didn't get involved in the EI effort.

If managers and employees do not have the opportunity to influence the changes, they may be limited or encapsulated by those who see little opportunity to shape the future direction. Participation by a broad spectrum of stakeholders in identifying issues and planning for their resolution is paramount to building the widespread commitment and support neeeded for success.

To increase involvement in and support of plans, many organizations have created several committees, composed of employees from all functions and levels, to help with the planning process. These committees will be discussed in Chapters Six and Seven.

IDENTIFYING A CORE GROUP

One of the first steps in changing or improving the way an organization functions requires that key people perceive the need for change and have a vision of how the organization should function. The first step toward this end often involves creating a core group. Beckhard defines a core group as individuals within an organization who are needed to bring about the desired change— that is, "people who can make it happen."[1]

A core group often consists of a key manager and staff. A key manager is one who heads an organizational entity, such as a company, division, department, function, manufacturing, or service facility, and has the authority to sanction a change effort and be accountable for its impact.

A number of factors help identify candidates for core group membership:

• Managers who can commit resources and provide some degree of protection from budget cuts and other restrictions imposed by

---

[1] Richard Beckhard and Reuben T. Harris, *Organizational Transitions/Managing Complex Change* (Reading, Mass.: Addison-Wesley Publishing, 1977).

company practices and policies, and who also can provide support in the beginning and while the effort progresses.

• People with enough independence and authority to try new ways of operating. Plant managers who are away from corporate offices frequently fit this criteria.

• People with foresight who are able to see new ways of working and want to change the way in which the organization functions.

• Specialists from human resources departments who have expertise in managing change or know where to obtain it.

• "Influence" leaders who can help spread the effort's successes.

Many participative efforts have been started by key managers at lower levels of an organization; but the efforts did not receive support from top management until after they had experienced success. Without eventual support from the top, these efforts usually lose momentum. Therefore, top management should be represented in the core group or at least be fully informed and supportive of core group efforts.

DEVELOPING UNDERSTANDING

Building understanding among key people in the organization about what a team-based organization is and what it can do is important for their commitment and support. This often can be accomplished through education.

Learn about Teams from Other Organizations. Visits to other organizations can prove to be a very useful way to learn how to plan and implement a team-based organization. The following questions are examples of the areas to explore:

1. What is the history of the effort?
   a. How and where did it start? (Top, bottom, a department, or division?)
2. What are the goals of the change effort and how do they fit with the business strategy?
   a. Have they linked the effort to business objectives? If so, how?

3. Is there an explicitly stated management philosophy? If so, how was it introduced, how is it reinforced and supported?

4. What role has senior management played in starting and maintaining the effort?

5. What role has middle management played in the change and do these managers have ownership in the effort?

6. What changes have taken place in leadership style, policies, and procedures to ensure consistency with the effort?

7. Does the union actively support the effort? If so, how? If not, why not?

8. Methods and extent of participation.
   a. What methods of involving employees has the organization used?
   b. What percentage of employees are actively participating?
   c. What is the reaction of those who are not yet actively participating in some facet of the effort? This means those who are not yet working in problem-solving groups or yet contributing in some way to planning and goal-setting in their work unit.

9. How have they dealt with issues of consistency and ground rules?
   a. Are all divisions or departments following the same approach and using the same methods and techniques?

10. What type of training has proven most effective?

11. Where has the most resistance occurred? Why? What has been done to reduce resistance?

12. To what extent is employee participation a standard operating procedure and not a special program?

13. What have been the biggest obstacles to overcome?

14. What factors have contributed the most to their success?

15. How long did it take to see tangible results?

16. Have they attempted to measure the cost and benefits? If so, how?

17. Has the effort contributed to:
    a. Employees contributing to higher quality and lower cost of products and services?
    b. Employees being more flexible and adaptable to change?
    c. Employee job satisfaction.
18. If they had the opportunity to start over, what would they do differently?

Attend Seminars. These would be presented by universities, organizations, or consultants and would provide the opportunity to hear about the efforts made by several companies representing many different industries.

Read. Included here are pertinent books, case studies, and articles to supplement the first-hand experience of visits and seminars.

Work with Consultants. Such people should possess the experience of implementing team-based organizations.

MANAGEMENT'S CONCERNS

Two key questions that frequently arise from managers who are about to undertake a team-based change effort are:

1. How can teams help accomplish the organization's goals?
2. What are the potential risks?

The potential benefits are:

- Higher productivity and improved quality of product or service—insofar as those can be achieved through greater teamwork and application of knowledge, skill, and brain power by the work force.
- A lasting improvement in the capabilities of the work force.
- An enhancement of employee dignity, self-esteem, and job satisfaction.

The potential risks are:

- Investment of money, time, and effort with little return.
- The emotional strain of getting an organization to behave differently.
- "Creating employee cynicism when attempts are only half-hearted or are not followed through."[2]

OVERCOMING RESISTANCE

Managers have been inclined to take the necessary risks to change—to the extent they recognize the need for a different way of operating—and see teams as a possible solution. The energy or drive to change frequently comes from dissatisfaction with the current state of affairs and a desire to change them.

This was certainly a strong motivation in the 1980s. This was a time when organizations were threatened by foreign competition and felt they needed to become more competitive.

Sometimes the drive for change is the result of a manager's vision of how the organization could function better, even though it is presently very profitable. These managers frequently have a harder time explaining to the organization, in a way that people can understand, why they are advocating a change. The attitude is "We are successful—why change?"

For example, an organization with several years of progressively higher profits has undertaken developing team-based organizations in a number of its manufacturing facilities. Some of the first facilities to undergo this changeover have been either less profitable or overall low performers, as measured by the corporation or greenfield—that is, new start-up situations.

Within this organization, some people view becoming a team-based organization as being what you do when you are in trouble. In fact, the employees of a "profitable" plant that has gone to teams have had difficulty understanding why they are changing.

---

[2] Jerome Rosow and Robert Zager, *Productivity through Work Innovations*, Work in America Institute (New York: Pergamon Press, 1982).

The management has steadfastly said "we" are changing to get better and continue to grow. For some, this message has been hard to hear.

The need to change when faced with an unprofitable situation or a threatened closing is easy to understand. Changing to get better or to improve is a visionary and essential stance—but be aware that it may be harder for employees and managers to understand.

To help overcome the resistance created by the perceived cost or risk of changing, clear goals and next steps must be established. First, however, it is necessary to identify why people are resistant to change in order to determine where to channel energies to develop support.

For example, education efforts that illustrate how the organization can be improved are indicated when people are satisfied with the present state of affairs and need to be made aware of better ways of operating. Efforts aimed at defining a desired future state are appropriate when clear goals for the change have not been defined. When the organization is struggling for survival, finding examples of what other organizations have done that were in a similar situation can be helpful to managers who are looking for some possible approaches to their already felt need.

Managers, at least those who prefer to maintain their traditional authority within the work force, frequently resist a change that may require more participative ways of managing. If widespread dissemination to a team-based operation is to take place, then significant changes may have to be made in the management philosophy. This may not always meet with the favorable reaction by members of the organization who do not want their jobs changed. They may feel threatened and become opponents of the team concept.

Managers need to see a significant role for themselves, and that managing teams requires their experience to make the organization function effectively. The manager's expertise and experience is taken advantage of through coaching and counseling the team. The appropriate management approach can range from providing directive leadership to observing and facilitating how the team functions.

Each team's needs for direction will vary depending on their skill level, experience, and the complexity of the task. The team leader's role will be described in more detail in Chapter Nine.

Frequently, the best tool for overcoming resistance is to encourage employees and managers who are resistant to talk with those employees within their organization who are in favor of the change, or with employees in other organizations who have experienced such a change. In doing so, they hear what others see as the benefits.

Talking with and visiting organizations that already have made a change also can be very helpful. They can see or hear first-hand what the problems and successes have been. Equally important, however, is the chance for those who resist to voice their concerns and feel that they have been heard and will have an opportunity to help shape the change effort to overcome their concerns.

LIMITS TO CHANGE

Early in the planning process it is important to develop a clear understanding of the limits to change and the likely impact of outside factors. Clarifying the boundaries usually reduces whatever tensions exist about how far the change will go and what will change.

The core group should discuss and determine if there are limits on the following issues:

1. Personnel, funding.
2. The latitude to change corporate-wide systems. For example, the compensation system may need to be changed to reward teams.
3. The latitude for experimentation. Specific issues for discussion include the latitude to impact company policy, management prerogative, and the union contract.
4. The core group should also consider what impact such external factors as national negotiations, mergers, and reorganizations may have on the change effort.

UNION INVOLVEMENT

In unionized organizations, the support, commitment, and active involvement of the union are important for success. In any unionized company, the employees have "hired" the union to represent them. If the union tells employees not to cooperate, many will not.

Experience has shown it is difficult to maintain an effective effort if the union resists participation. The best efforts tend to arise from joint union/management commitment. This is best exemplified through joint planning and implementation.

In the early planning stages with one organization, my colleagues and I informed management that we felt, given the circumstances, the union should be jointly involved in the change effort. Management's response was that it would inform the union of what it decided and then give the union an opportunity to voice concerns.

As consultants, we pointed out their approach was no different than past behavior and would probably not gain the support that the managers desired from the union. After much discussion, management held fast to its point of view.

As part of educating the management on what other companies have done, we suggested the managers attend an Organization Development Network Conference, because several companies were presenting what they had done about their change efforts.

On their return, a member of management said, "I guess you must be right about involving the union." Other managers reiterated how companies that presented information at the conference stressed the need for union involvement.

Having crossed over that hurdle, the next step was to approach the union to ask for its joint involvement in planning and implementing the change effort. The union president and officers were invited to a meeting where management laid out the proposal for a joint employee involvement effort. The union members' response was to cross their arms, push themselves slightly back from the conference table, and say, "You tell us what you want to do and we will tell you if we agree." They were assuming the same stance that management originally wanted for them.

Historically, unions have reacted to management plans and decisions, and their constituents have seen them as their defenders when management decisions are viewed unfavorably. This stance has allowed unions to be highly visible and active advocates for their constituents. The emerging union role has been to work with managements as co-planners, decision makers, and implementers.

As a co-planner of change, unions become involved in decisions and plans as these are being developed. The unions predetermine the impact on their constituents and work with management to develop the best approach. This role establishes the union along with management as an advocate of a decision or of a point of view. This can be a very uncomfortable position for unions, especially on controversial issues.

There always will be opportunities for trade-offs between the long-term welfare of employees and the organization. Union and management will need to work together to ensure the welfare of both.

The role of planner is not always highly visible to constituents. Consequently, union leaders may be concerned that their membership may not know what they are doing and how they are influencing decisions. The union's new role should be communicated frequently, if it is to be understood and supported. Some organizations have either added or rotated a few employees through the various planning committees, so they can communicate to others how the committees work and about the union's role.

Increasing employee understanding of and input into decisions that affect them greatly reduces the union's risk of being seen as in collusion with management. As employees become more involved in decisions that affect their work, it becomes more obvious that union and management are working together to benefit everyone.

Management made several more efforts to explain that it wanted to change the old way of working and to work more closely together in planning and implementing change. The more management talked, the firmer the union became in its position. Finally, the union agreed to think about the proposal and talk further with the consultants, as well as with other unions who had been involved in such efforts.

During the meeting with the consultants, the union challenged who we were working for. We responded that our work so far had been with management; but, under the joint proposal, we would work with a joint union/management steering committee. When asked who was paying us, we responded the company; but, if the union wished, a joint fund could be established to pay our fees. We also made it clear that we were consultants to the joint committee.

The next question was what in this approach was for the union. Rather than trying to sell them, we jointly discussed the pros and cons of a joint venture. After several more meetings between management and the union, where they (both) laid out the ground rules and safeguards, the union finally agreed to a joint effort.

This is not a decision that the organization could make quickly. The surfacing of concerns by all parties and the development of ground rules and safeguards was key in the union reaching an agreement. Finally, the focus on the win/win goals of product quality and employee job satisfaction were rallying points that all could support.

Union support may vary, depending on its early experience. In many organizations, successes have led to strong support by union and management. However, some organizations have had "false starts"—that is, efforts not living beyond one year. This causes union leadership to view any attempt to change as just another management gimmick that doesn't work.

Unions may actively oppose participative efforts if it views them as management efforts to alienate employees from the union, with the ultimate objective of destroying the union. Unions must be satisfied that the converse is true, and management must demonstrate this attitude by involving the union in the goal setting, planning, and implementation. Ford Motor

Company and the UAW addressed the need for union support by creating a joint labor/management committee, which established the ground rules of the EI effort, and which developed the plans and led the way for implementation throughout the organization.

Both management and union must be educated about the benefits to the company, to the employees, and to the union. Management and union leaders must be committed to using every employee's talents to the fullest extent possible and to making the organization a better place to work. The union cannot be committed only to the human outcomes, nor can management seek only economic outcomes.

Implementing a team-based change may require a new pay system or a redefining of jobs or other actions that will impact the bargaining agreement. To allow such experimentation, a moratorium may need to be established on some aspects of management rights or the union contract, especially if the contract so tightly defines what can and cannot be done that any change would be a violation.

A moratorium requires trust and must be clearly specified in written agreements. The moratorium agreement should provide sufficient protection to allow all parties to feel comfortable but be flexible enough for an acceptable level of change to evolve. Such a document should state that change can take place, providing the following conditions are met.

1. Changes in normally established practices can be made only within the agreed-upon part of the organization.
2. Expansion of these practices will take place only after being tested for a suitable period and with total agreement by all parties.
3. Either party has veto power over the change and can rescind the new practices after the agreed-upon time has expired for the first phase.

However, a point of no return—that is, a point when the changes cannot be rescinded—should be agreed upon. This keeps the change from being used by either party as a bargaining chip, and it encourages employees and management to fully participate in supporting the changes.

Both parties must realize the potential difficulty in rescinding the practices that employees have found productive and rewarding. Therefore, before agreeing to proceed, they should feel confident they can support the change and be willing to consider changing the labor contract if needed.

Managers need to be sensitive about how the planning and implementation might change in an organization that is not represented by a union. For example, who speaks for the employees? It is frequently necessary to get a large number of employees who represent a wide range of functions and opinions involved in the planning. Furthermore, these employees will need to be encouraged to speak their opinions, and management must be prepared to listen.

All-employee surveys can help to identify opinions and assure employees that their views are being solicited. Obviously, their opinions should be either acted on or reasons given why other approaches were taken.

Other matters, such as steering committee membership and how members are chosen, may differ in a union or non-union organization. The selection of a steering committee will be covered in Chapter Six.

EMPLOYEES' ROLE

In many organizations, employees are frequently in the position of reacting to decisions and plans. Being a member of a team provides opportunities for them to be more actively involved in decision making and planning, which, in turn, creates a willingness to be committed to the mutually agreed-upon actions. This is a significant change.

Under the old system, unsatisfactory decisions could be appealed. Under the new system, rather than appealing an action, employees—along with management and the union—take some of the responsibility for decisions and, if needed, alter them. This requires viewing decisions within a larger context, and employees need to be much more informed and aware of all the pros and cons of a course of action, if they are to take a win/win perspective in influencing or making decisions.

THE ROLE OF POLICY

The development up front of a policy or management philosophy supporting teamwork can help launch and ensure a change effort's success. Policies help shape the environment and maintain organizations in a "stable state" by ensuring that certain practices persist.[3] Increased participation may begin to challenge existing policies and encourage change.

At the same time, permanent change may require the creation of new policies, procedures, and processes to ensure that the new way of operating becomes standard. A policy or statement about teamwork makes it a permanent way of life instead of a current fad.

For example, the following 1979 letter of understanding between Ford and the UAW was intended to make employee involvement a permanent entity versus a passing fad.

> Employee involvement holds promise for aiding and expanding efforts of the company and the union to make work a more satisfying and stimulating experience. Constructive efforts to involve employees to a greater degree in relevant workplace matters may also enhance employee creativity, contribute to improvements in the workplace, support goals of achieving the highest quality products, heighten efficiency, and reduce unwarranted absenteeism.
>
> Projects involving represented employees require consultation between their union representatives and local managements, and they contain the potential for improving the overall work environment. Such efforts thereby will benefit the company by contributing to increased employee job satisfaction and a reduction in employee absenteeism and turnover, and benefit consumers through improvement in the overall quality of products and services.[4]

---

[3] Donald Schon, *Beyond the Stable State* (New York: Random House, 1971).

[4] Ford Motor Company and the UAW Letter of Understanding, October 4, 1979.

Within your organization, management and the union may or may not believe a policy or a negotiated agreement is necessary. However, as a minimum, there should be considerable discussion and a complete understanding and agreement on the direction and intent of the change, and on how it will affect the existing bargaining relationship.

GUIDELINES/GROUND RULES

Establishing guidelines can help to set limits on the extent of experimentation. Over time, these guidelines can be altered to allow either more or less risk taking.

Guidelines act much like the rules of an athletic game: They provide a safe boundary in which all parties can fully participate once they know the limits. Both union and management will feel more comfortable if they know that past agreements will not be violated.

The more the union and employees help define and understand the rules, the more fully they will accept and participate in the change process. Guidelines also contribute to creating a feeling that there is equity in the process and that all parties will play by the rules. They ensure "due process," so problems can be mutually resolved to everyone's satisfaction.

In one organization that has a joint union/management effort, frequent meetings have been called to discuss guideline infractions. The one guideline that has made these meetings possible and productive stated that, "All disputes will be discussed and resolved to both parties's satisfaction. Disputes are not a basis for ending the joint effort."

The development of guidelines also serves as an educational and team-building experience. As members develop guidelines, they exchange ideas and open up communications. This process helps to develop a mutual image of the future changes that might be considered.

DETERMINING WHERE TO START

Managers frequently want to begin where they are having the greatest difficulty. The areas where they are having the most difficulty also often contain the least-skilled management and the worst working conditions. Wanting to improve these areas may be a valid reason for undertaking an effort there. However, these areas are not optimal places to start.

Starting an effort where managers and employees are having difficulty coping day to day may not give the change effort the running start it needs to take hold and flourish. Unsuccessful first efforts may eliminate the opportunity for a second chance. Many organizations start where the probability of early success is the greatest. Difficult areas are addressed later.

If you choose to start in one area and expand the results, instead of totally redesigning the organization, the following criteria have been used by other organizations to help them determine where to start their efforts. These are targets for which to aim. The likelihood of meeting all criteria varies considerably by organization. Use them as guidelines to help ensure success in your early efforts.

Criteria

Skilled Management and Union

Management and union representatives should be skilled in dealing with people and also have a positive track record. You wouldn't start the implementation of an important new marketing approach with your least-qualified people. Therefore, it doesn't make sense to start implementing a team-based organization with your least-qualified personnel.

Many managers frequently want to correct their worst problems first, or they want to give this "new approach" the acid test. Team-based organizations are not a cure-all for poor or unskilled management.

High Probability of Success[5]

The likelihood of success, of course, will be determined by many of these criteria. However, most organizations have an intuitive feel about whether the area has a high probability of success, based on its past performance and past experience in implementing changes.

High Potential for Diffusion of Results[6]

There is usually higher acceptance of the initial results if the area selected has some similarities to other parts of the organization. If people feel the area selected is unique or isolated from the rest of the organization, or that anyone could be successful in that area but the results cannot be applied to the larger organization, it probably is not the best place to start.

The success of General Foods's Topeka plant was at first discounted by other parts of the organization, because it was a new facility, with a small, single-focus product, and in a labor market where the plant had a choice of the top workers. Obviously, these circumstances helped Topeka's success.

When companies select the second area for change, that area tends to find reasons why they are different from the first, and, therefore, what was done will not apply to them.

In some ways they are right—they are different. However, the general approach of giving teams the responsibility to operate their areas has been successful in a myriad of organizations and different situations.

For example, a plant manager who had been instrumental in implementing and managing a high involvement organization relayed the following story. While attending a seminar of plant managers from various industries who were also managing similar high involvement or team-based organizations, each was asked to write the answer to how large an organization must be so such work could be successful.

---

[5] T. G. Cummings, "Sociotechnical Systems: An Intervention Strategy," in *Sociotechnical Systems; A Sourcebook*, by William Passmore and John J. Sherwood (La Jolla, Calif.: University Associates, 1978), p. 171.

[6] Ibid.

Each wrote the size of their plant. The attendees came from plants of less than 100 to over 1,000. Each manager felt his or her situation was unique and that it would be difficult or impossible to do what each had done in a larger organization.

To help apply the good ideas from the initial start-up areas, managers and employees from the second and subsequent areas that start up, should be involved with the planning of the change in the first area. First efforts should not be called experiments but, rather, phase one. Experiment connotes that the effort may fail and that the area is unique.

Employees and the Leadership Are Interested in Working Together [7]

Employees and the leadership must be interested in trying new ways of relating and cooperating. Sometimes the relationships are so strained and the trust levels so low that people are reluctant to try new ways of interacting.

An approach that has worked well in several organizations is to encourage employees and managers to take small steps toward working together. As they find a step to be successful, they are more willing to take on bigger issues.

I frequently have interviewed both managers and employees to identify what they would like to see changed to make their work area more productive and be a more satisfying place to work. When the results are shared, everyone can see that they want similar things. The feedback of the interview results is followed by a meeting of employees and managers to begin talking about how these things can be achieved. When people see that progress, although slow, can be made, they have been willing to invest more of their talents and energies toward working together.

The following example of work with a manager and his team illustrates how relationships can change if they experience small successes. Here the manager asked for help to build the team and its relationship with him.

He was concerned that the team would not take on the responsibilities that had been identified for it by a group of its peers. The

---

[7] Ibid.

team was concerned that management would not give it the freedom and authority to take on the responsibilities.

The action steps to resolve this included interviews with all members of the team and management and a joint three-day meeting to discuss the results. The meeting started slowly, because everyone was reluctant to talk about their concerns. However, when they did talk they were able to make progress.

On the third day, one of the employees said, "If management would give us the freedom to perform these responsibilities, we can greatly improve this operation." Management responded with, "That's exactly what we want also." They agreed to start small and slow at the next team meeting by having the team run the meeting.

The feedback by the managers after the next meeting was that it was a great meeting and that their job was getting easier. The feedback from the employee who led the meeting was that it always goes well when "we" can be in charge of our area.

Working as a Team Will Make a Difference in Organization Effectiveness or in Employee Satisfaction

Sometimes outside forces control these outcomes and teamwork has little impact. A call I received one day from a manager of a manufacturing facility illustrates how outside influences can overshadow what a team can do.

He wanted help in building his management team. He related some recent problems that told him his team was not working well together. They had several extra boxcars of raw materials that they were not able to use. They also had hired 300 extra people and laid them off the following week.

Upon further looking into these problems, I discovered none of the decisions that caused these problems were either made by or within the control of the manager's team. Corporate marketing had planned a major new product introduction but cancelled it and forgot to inform the plant management.

The issues were outside the control of the team. The team needed to learn how to better manage its interaction with outside factors. In this particular case, to manage future product introductions and general interactions between corporate functions and the plant, an expanded team was created consisting of members from the corporate functions and plant management.

Interdependence

The interdependence or linkage of work areas can affect the choice of where to start. By starting at the beginning of the work process, problems can be corrected with minimum need for involvement by areas involved in later stages of the process. However, if you start at the end of a series of interdependent work areas—for example, an assembly line—the work coming out of the first department may impact on subsequent departments, and their ability to make changes.

To illustrate, poor quality or improper assembly early in the line can affect the work of people further down the line. Starting at the middle or end of the process immediately draws in preceding departments and those that supply materials and assistance. We will discuss further how to deal with interdependence in deciding how to put together teams in Chapter Seven.

READINESS PLANNING

Readiness planning can be helpful to identify areas on which to focus when preparing for a change effort. It is important, though, to remember that few organizations are ever totally ready for change. Therefore, a low rating on the following questions should not be interpreted as a deterrent but merely as an indication of where more work is required. The Readiness Planning Questionnaire is intended to encourage discussion on how to proceed with an effort, to identify areas requiring change, and to help determine the scope of the change effort.

Completing the Questionnaire

The core group should complete the questionnaire and discuss the results.

Readiness Planning Questionnaire

Instructions: Put a *P* next to the description that best fits the organization's *present* state and an *F* next to the description that best fits the desired *future* state in two or three years. You may want to create your own description if none fits your situation.

1. Management's understanding and support of the need to change.

1	2	3	4
Poor understanding; no visible support.	Little understanding; token support.	Fair understanding; some visible support.	Thorough understanding; commitment.

Reasons: _____

_____

_____

2. Unions' understanding and support of the need to change.

1	2	3	4
Poor understanding; no visible support.	Little understanding; token support.	Fair understanding; some visible support.	Thorough understanding; commitment.

Reasons: _____

_____

_____

3. Top management goals for change.

1	2	3	4
Long-term goals unclear, short-term goal is cost reduction.	Limited goal definition and appreciation for long-term benefits.	Some goals defined; interest in long-term benefits for the organization and employees.	Goals clear: committed to long-term increase in organization effectiveness and job satisfaction.

Reasons: _____

_____

_____

4. Union goals for change.

1	2	3	4
Long-term goals unclear, short-term goal is cost reduction.	Limited goal definition and appreciation for long-term benefits.	Some goals defined; interest in long-term benefits for the organization and employees.	Goals clear: committed to long-term increase in organization effectiveness and job satisfaction.

Reasons: _____

_____

_____

5. Benefits of increasing employee involvement in planning and decision making.

1	*2*	*3*	*4*
No perceived benefit.	Little benefit.	Moderate benefit.	High benefit.

Reasons: _____

_____

_____

6. Middle management's attitude toward change.

1	*2*	*3*	*4*
Fear; resent turning over company to employees.	Cautious; concerned about threat to managers' authority.	Interested in trying.	Eager to sponsor and be involved.

Reasons: _____

_____

_____

7. Union representatives' attitudes toward change.

1	*2*	*3*	*4*
Fear; resent turning over company to employees.	Cautious; concerned about threat to the reps.' authority.	Interested in trying.	Eager to sponsor and be involved.

Reasons: _____

_____

_____

8. Supervisors' and managers' interpersonal communications and team management skills.

1	2	3	4
Generally poor; no opportunity to apply.	Fair; limited opportunity to apply.	Good; supported by training and various opportunities to apply.	Excellent; consistent effort at all levels on developing and applying skills.

Reasons: _____

_____

_____

9. Commitment of resources.

1	2	3	4
No dollars or staffing available.	Assign task as an additional duty and to do within current budget.	Some staff and seed money can be spared on a trial basis.	High-potential line managers are available full time. Budget exists for change effort.

Reasons: _____

_____

_____

10. Training.

1	2	3	4
No time for training.	Train only the people directly involved in teams.	Train teams and management.	Training is an ongoing essential way of operating for everyone.

Reasons: _____

_____

_____

11. Commitment to a realistic time frame.

1	*2*	*3*	*4*
Expect results to immediately exceed costs.	Expect results to exceed costs within one year.	Expect results to exceed costs within two or three years.	Expect results to exceed costs when the change becomes an ongoing part of company culture.

Reasons: _____

_____

_____

12. Organizational continuity and predictability.

1	*2*	*3*	*4*
Constant; major organizational changes or layoffs likely.	Possible organizational changes or layoffs.	Predictable future direction; little likelihood of organizational changes or layoffs.	Stable; specific effort made to insure continuity.

Reasons: _____

_____

_____

13. History of change efforts.

1	2	3	4
Just another program; everyone is waiting for it to eventually disappear.	Perfunctory participation and support; little long-term effect.	Earlier efforts somewhat supported and successful.	Earlier efforts supported and very successful.

Reasons: _____

_____

_____

14. Employee's support.

1	2	3	4
Highly skeptical; will not support.	Somewhat skeptical; wait and see.	Willing to give it a try.	Eager to get started; highly supportive.

Reasons: _____

_____

_____

15. General comments. _____

_____

_____

_____

_____

_____

_____

Analzying Results

After each individual member completes the questionnaire, a summary of all ratings should be tabulated. Each individual should retain a copy of his or her responses, to compare them to the summary. Each item in the summary should be discussed, to determine the current state of the organization and where it should be in two or three years. The discussions should focus on where the group members want the organization to be in the future, what has to change to get there, and next steps.

The chances for a successful change effort are greater when the *now* responses are closer to a "four." The decisions made and actions planned should be with the intent of moving the future organization closer to level four, although this does not mean that all organizations eventually must be at this level.

SUMMARY

The planning and early assumptions and decisions that have been made can greatly affect a team-based change effort. Management should thoroughly analyze its situation to determine its readiness and how to proceed. Identifying and planning to resolve the union's, management's and employee's issues, are paramount to a successful effort. After deciding what issues need to be addressed to create a team-based organization, the next step is to develop the method for designing and implementing the new organization.

Chapter Six

Organization Evolution

DESIGN A NEW ORGANIZATION OR EVOLVE

There are two frequently used approaches to developing a team-based organization. One approach, which I call "organization evolution," emerged from the quality of work life and the employee involvement work of the 1970s and 1980s. During these efforts, organizations formed problem-solving teams to improve quality and organization effectiveness, and to increase employee participation.

When problem-solving teams were operating effectively, the next step was to form natural work teams and to gradually increase their autonomy until they could manage their work area.

The second approach, which had its beginnings in newly created operations, involves commissioning a design team to design either a part or a total organization. The team determines the organization structure, the number of levels, the makeup of the teams, the jobs the teams perform, and the systems necessary to support teamwork. The second approach will be covered in Chapter Seven. This chapter will cover the issues to address in managing the evolution to a team-based organization.

Changing existing organizations usually involves some evolution and some redesign. It is difficult to change everything at once. Likewise, it is important to examine the organization as a design team would do—to determine what is needed before evolving. Therefore, the change processes in many organizations have been hybrids of the two methods to be described. They have been separated in this book to more easily explain each.

A newly created organization has the option of designing the structure and work processes in the way it chooses. Existing organizations, however, must find ways to so alter its structure, processes, and organizational culture that the ways are supportive of teams. The concepts covered in this book apply to new as well as existing organizations. The emphasis, however, will be upon change in existing organizations; therefore, see Figure 6–1 before your sojourn.

The *evolution approach* may seem safer or less risky but can result in teams that become encapsulated. For example, some members of the organization may perceive the starting of teams in one area as a way of delaying their involvement, with the hope that the effort will fail before it reaches them. Limiting the initial effort to one area also may create a pent-up demand—that is, employees in other parts of the organization may want to be involved before the organization is ready.

The *design approach* can seem very risky and requires considerable commitment and faith that whatever is designed will work. This approach encourages changes on an organization-wide basis and deals up front with the areas outlined in the teamwork foundation in Chapter Two.

However you approach moving toward a greater use of teams, processes should be established that allow employees to influence the new direction. It is important to have employee feedback about each phase of the change process, and that the approach decided upon takes this feedback into consideration. Without this last step, team-based approaches to improve organizational effectiveness may be viewed as rigid management programs and not receive the employee support needed for implementation.

In one organization that keeps employees informed through meetings, it sends up trial balloons. The company also leaks infor-

---

FIGURE 6–1

Common Approaches to Building a Team-Based Organization

Employee Involvement Evolution	*Design a New Organization*
A core group decides to undertake a team-based EI effort and develops a vision.	A core group decides to design a team-based organization and develops a vision.
↓	↓
A steering committee is educated.	A design team is educated.
↓	↓
A steering committee develops an implementation plan.	A design team develops a proposal for the new organization, including an implementation strategy.
↓	
Problem-solving teams meet and make recommendations.	
↓	↓
The number of teams is expanded and team autonomy is increased.	Implementation of design by line organization.
↓	↓
Continual modifications and improvement.	Continual modifications and improvement.

---

mation, much like a press leak, to get employees' responses to the ideas. In addition, the company spends considerable time involving employees in the planning of change. The result has been that employees feel informed and able to influence the changes through the formal planning process and through their feedback on the company's trial balloons and information leaks.

PARALLEL ORGANIZATION

Sometimes organizations need to create parallel structures in the form of committees to initiate and expedite change. I am frequently approached by managers who are having difficulty understanding why participative approaches to managing organizations don't rapidly evolve or quickly take hold. They often say, "Supervisors have been given what they have asked for: more authority. Employees have had input. Why don't supervisors take charge? Why don't employees get involved? Perhaps they need more training."

Usually, the search for solutions to these dilemmas center on what managers think are deficiencies on the part of supervisors or employees, rather than on the hierarchical system in which they work. Oshry speaks of supervisors as "middles" caught between higher management and employees, and who often are viewed by upper management as weak, unskilled, and unsupportive.[1] Since most organizations do not make a habit of hiring supervisors with this profile, the reasons for their inabilities, therefore, must reside in the hierarchical system itself.

The expectations of management and employees begin to define the supervisors' role and shape their behavior. Therefore, rather than looking for simple training solutions, look at what behavior the organization encourages. Ask "What are the recurring problems telling us?"

Since there are many answers, training by itself is seldom an adequate solution. Instead, more fundamental changes usually are needed in how the organization functions. The changes might include involving supervisors in decisions that affect them, redefining their roles, levels of authority, making information available, and allowing them greater influence on what happens in the organization. As described in Chapter Four, the organization's structure, procedures, and processes must be addressed to ensure that they support what you want to create.

Trying to bring about change without modifying structures and processes is like teaching someone to swim without providing a pool. There is no reinforcement or building of a more supportive organization for the desired change. Experiences with training groups in the 1950s and 1960s revealed that personal change on

---

[1] B. Oshry, *Middles of the World, Integrate* (New York: Power and Systems, Inc., 1982).

the job must be reinforced by organizational norms, practices, policies, structures, or processes for the change to be permanent. Many employees who tried to change after a training experience and found the culture unsupportive often either reverted back to old behaviors or left the organization. Effective transfer of new behaviors to the workplace requires reinforcement and support.

Schon contends that the core nature of an organization must be altered to change the way in which it functions.[2] For example, allowing changes in such things as dress did not fundamentally alter how the military functions. However, changing the hierarchical structure and distribution of authority would have a great impact.

A common strategy for gradually changing the core nature of organizations and also providing support for the changes has been the parallel organization. A structure composed of steering and implementation committees and problem-solving teams "parallels" the formal organization. The formal organization primarily is designed to make decisions with some level of consistency and predictability; it is designed to be stable and to produce a product or service.

For the most part, organizations are very effective at doing this. However, they often are not as effective in the following areas:

1. Handling deviations from the norm.
2. Encouraging upward communications and high participation.
3. Identifying and developing creative solutions to existing problems.
4. Finding ways to improve the organization's effectiveness by changing its very nature.

Since the formal organization frequently is not designed for the above purposes, it doesn't focus its energies and attention on them. "The task of the parallel organization is to continually ex-

---

[2] Donald A. Schon, *Beyond the Stable State* (New York: Random House, 1971).

plore new ways of operating. It seeks to institutionalize change."[3] The parallel organization focuses its energies and attention toward processes that renew an organization and increase its effectiveness. It allows experimentation with new behaviors, such as increased creativity, problem solving, and information exchange. It also becomes the vehicle for transferring what is learned to the formal structure.

As a result of experimenting with new ways of operating, the parallel organization makes recommendations for change that often require the formal organization to behave differently. Frequently, this can be threatening to the formal structure, especially if higher levels of management greet the recommendations with comments like "Why haven't supervisors solved that problem?"

If the initial recommendations are received negatively, the energy created by forming these committees will dissipate or find other ways to be released, and these can be destructive. Instead, the energy should be managed by encouraging new ideas and better ways to operate.

In a parallel structure, problem-solving team recommendations go through the formal organization for approval, since the intent of the change effort is not to bypass line managers in making daily decisions. However, if groups of employees feel their recommendations consistently are being rejected, an appeal process may be in order.

In one organization, an appeal process exists and its very presence indicates to managers and employees that good ideas will be considered, regardless of their origin. In fact, very few appeals are ever needed.

The success of the parallel organization at finding better ways to operate does not mean the formal structure is inadequate. Everyone must be able to share in the success of the two structures as they operate side by side. There always will be trade-offs between the reliability and predictability of the formal organization

---

[3] Barry Stein and Kanter Rosebeth, "Building the Parallel Organization: Creating Mechanisms for Permanent Quality of Work Life," *Journal of Applied Behavioral Science* 16, (1980), pp. 371–86.

and the uncertainty and change created by the parallel organization. Management must learn to use what is good within the formal organization and to change what can be made more effective.

Organizations initially designed for high involvement build many of the attributes of a parallel organization into the formal structure. They have constant employee meetings, with feedback of ideas and concerns, and they constantly examine how the organization functions to determine if it can be improved. To the extent this can be done in existing organizations, the parallel structure is less needed. In fact, there is the advantage of quicker change if organizations move from low to high participation without having to create a parallel structure.

This usually requires some up-front restructuring, such as fewer levels, and organizing work around teams and making changes in the reward, decision-making, planning, and communications systems. Most organizations that have been in existence for some time see this as too large a step, and they start with problem-solving teams and not with more autonomous work teams. They choose to move gradually toward higher levels of involvement.

In one major manufacturing operation, the plant manager constantly looks for opportunities to bring daily operations more in line with the "vision." When job openings occurred, he implemented a selection process that had employee committees within the department selecting new hires and transfers. This was seen as a first step toward teams doing their own hiring.

A parallel structure has a number of committees to guide the change. The purpose of involving committees in planning and implementing a team-based change effort is threefold.

First, the committees provide many ideas from as wide a range of functions and levels in the organization as possible. This ensures that all points of view are heard in putting together the new organization.

Second, they ensure that, if one or two key people leave the organization, there are additional people who have been involved in the change to carry it on, so the change is not subject to the influence of a few people.

Three, by involving large segments of the organization's population in planning the change, not only is the product better but the likelihood of acceptance is increased. People tend to accept what they have helped to create.

The following, Figure 6–2, is one example of how an organization has used committees in a parallel organization. The number of committees and levels you might have will depend upon the complexity of your organization.

Companies have used many titles for committees. The following diagram and definitions, in Figure 6–3, are an attempt to simplify the responsibilities and relationship of one to another. Some

---

FIGURE 6–2
Parallel Organization

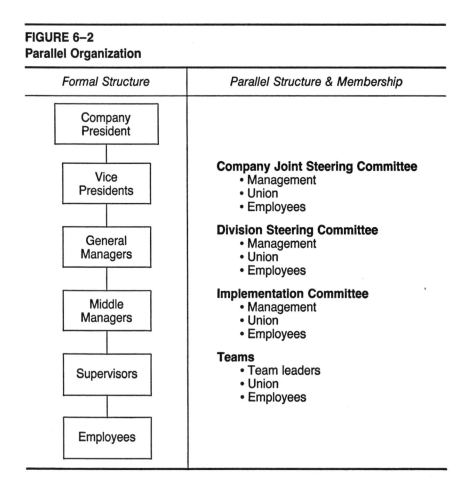

Formal Structure	*Parallel Structure & Membership*
Company President	
Vice Presidents	**Company Joint Steering Committee** • Management • Union • Employees
General Managers	**Division Steering Committee** • Management • Union • Employees
Middle Managers	**Implementation Committee** • Management • Union • Employees
Supervisors	**Teams** • Team leaders • Union • Employees
Employees	

FIGURE 6–3
Parallel Organization Committees

Committee	Membership	Function
Core Group	Top management and union.	Commission the change effort and provide overall direction and resources. In some organizations, there is no steering committee; the core group performs its function.
Steering Committee	Cross-section of management, union, and employees. In some organizations, several or all members of the core group are on the committee.	Working committee, which addresses the planning of the change strategy and monitoring progress.
Design Team	Diagonal cross-section of the organization.	Design the organization structure and systems. Design teams can be used in the newly created as well as in the evolving organizations.
Implementation Team	Management in the area of implementation plus members of the design team from the area.	Develop implementation plans and implement.
Work Team	Actual work team.	Run work area on daily basis.
Problem-solving Team	Actual work team or selected members of one or more work teams.	Solve problems in work area.

organizations have combined the responsibilities of several committees into one. This depiction of committees is not meant to be a recommendation.

Organizations that plan to evolve to self-managing teams by way of problem-solving teams have had the following configuration of committees. When organization design issues have emerged, they have been handled by the core group or the steering committee, or a design team is assembled.

- Core group.
- Steering committee.
- Implementation committee.
- Problem-solving/work teams.

In these organizations, a coordinator works with the committees as an internal consultant, and the supervisor or a facilitator helps teams with their process. These roles will be explained in Chapter Nine.

Companies that choose to redesign the organization typically have had the following committees:

- Core groups.
- Design team.
- Implementation committee.
- Work team.

In these organizations, the coordinator works as an internal consultant with the committees and the facilitator, who is often the previous supervisor, works with the work team.

In this organization, the facilitator is often the previous supervisor who works with the work team.

STEERING COMMITTEE

The steering committee usually is composed of people familiar with the work area. To provide continuity and long-term support, steering committee membership usually includes at least some of the original core group and, in fact, could be the core group with the addition of others.

The existence of a steering committee distributes responsibility, so the effort does not depend on just one person. Major change efforts require time and continuity of leadership for success. Lack of continuity can occur with personnel changes in management and union ranks. By distributing responsibility throughout the organization, continuity is ensured when individuals leave.

In addition to distributing responsibility, a steering committee has symbolic value. It communicates to the organization a serious commitment to something new and different.

There are advantages and disadvantages to creating a committee to guide an effort to increase participation. If the committee does not contain key managers, they may not understand the effort or feel that they have had enough influence on its nature. The obvious result is low commitment and poor implementation.

Conversely, if time is not set aside from the ongoing task of turning out widgets, and employees from various levels are not on committees, it is difficult to be as creative as needed about how to improve the process of making widgets. The result may be less employee input and creativity.

The steering committee plans the change strategy to fit the organization and monitors how it is working. As implied by the title, it steers the process to assure the highest level of involvement in and acceptance of the planned changes. It plays a key role in initiating the effort, in understanding how the change process is working, and in planning how to overcome resistance when it emerges.

However, the steering committee does not implement the strategy on a daily basis, because that would reduce the opportunity for all of management and employees to influence the direction and implementation of the change. The committee walks a fine line between being the planners and initiators of the change effort and not usurping line management's responsibilities of supporting and implementing the effort.

As the effort matures, usually during a period of years, the steering committee's role, as it has in some organizations, should be absorbed by the formal organization. There always may be a need, however, for some diagonal representation on a committee that periodically examines "how we're doing" and "where we should be going." Herein lies the dilemma. Without committees and parallel organizations, it is difficult to get a major change effort started. With them, it is sometimes difficult to get management at all levels to feel responsible for and make the changes.

Steering committees tend to be focused on and, therefore, creative about the type of change needed and to be innovative about how to bring it about. However, as an entity, they have little or no day-to-day responsibility for running the organization. Thus, they have a very low ability to implement the changes.

The formal organization, which tends to focus on the daily running of the business, is not as focused on change, rather on keeping things running. Conversely, however, since the formal organization is responsible for day-to-day operations, it has a high ability to implement change. The approach that has been most successful is to use committees to plan change and the formal organization to implement it.

Ultimately, to move to a highly involving organization, where employees are planning and making decisions about their work, requires either a partial or complete dismantling of the parallel structure and the assuming of its duties by the formal structure. Although the parallel organization may be necessary to get started, eventually its function must become the responsibility of every manager and employee.

What the parallel organization sets into motion must be taken over by the formal organization. There will always be a need for parallel planning groups that look for new ways of operating. However, these groups become more ad hoc; they perform their planning function and are reassimilated into the formal organization.

Steering Committee Role

A steering committee's role typically includes making recommendations and decisions in the following areas:

- Recommending the goals and scope of the change.
- Deciding the steps and methods for organizational assess-

ment—that is, determining how effectively the present organization is operating and how it should change. This is usually either done through employee surveys or interviews.

- Working with consultants and resources to develop change strategies that are most appropriate for the organization.
- Determining the type and extent of training and education that is required for members of the organization to support the effort.
- Determining resources required to implement the changes.
- Working with implementation committees to develop implementation plans.
- Recommending the pace of implementation.
- Overseeing expansion of initial efforts to other parts of the organization and preparing progress reports.
- Evaluating the effectiveness of the changes.
- Stimulating the development of new procedures and work processes.

Early in the change effort, steering committees allocate most of their time and attention to establishing and making increased involvement work. They provide training for management, supervisors, and employees and intervene when support is needed to ensure progress. Eventually, they must step back from these implementation tasks to evaluate the following issues:

- How the overall change process is working and whether adjustments are required.
- Whether patterns have emerged that signal the need for changes in organization-wide policies, practices, structures, and processes.

The role of steering committees evolves over time to one of making recommendations for organizational changes based upon the needs identified. Participative team efforts will cause a reexamination of how the organization should operate and what the appropriate management philosophy, work processes, and organization structure should be. All parties must understand that increasing team autonomy requires an evolution from a control to a commitment way of working.

Failure to respond to signals that indicate the need for change to support a higher level of involvement frequently will result in employee disillusionment, stagnation, or even termination of the effort. There will be continual choices to make in moving to a higher level of autonomy. When choices are made, steering committees and management must communicate clearly to the organization why they have elected to accept or reject moving to a higher level of involvement.

Steering Committee Membership

Similar to core group membership, the membership of the steering committee should consist of people who can make change happen through their influence, authority, power, and capability to ensure success. Committee members should provide access to key areas and levels within the organization. This usually requires the involvement of high levels of management and union.

If top levels are not on the committee, they should be kept well informed and agree with the committee's direction. This is the responsibility of the liaison person on the committee, who is also frequently a member of top management.

Where employees are not represented by a union, a process usually is set up that allows employees to select who they feel will do the best job. Attention must be given to ensuring that the various employee groupings feel that their views are adequately covered by the committee membership.

Having employees from all levels on the committee provides input that otherwise would not be available. This signals to the organization that all levels will be able to influence the direction of the change effort. Employees selected should be aware of the feelings and beliefs of co-workers and be willing to speak up in the presence of managers. They should be individuals who can interface with the rest of the organization and have credibility when they take the positions of the committee back to their groups.

The "ultimate" form of participation by employees for which

the organization is striving is not participation on the steering committee. The ultimate is employee participation in the daily planning and decision making in their work area. Employees should be well enough represented on the steering committee to successfully accomplish the ultimate goal. Committees, however, should be cognizant that too large a size makes decision making more difficult.

Since a small group can deal with issues more effectively, it is best keeping the size of the steering committee to approximately 10 to facilitate planning and decision making. Expanding beyond that number makes it more difficult to get a consensus decision and move ahead as rapidly as needed. Even so, it always is possible to add members or temporarily expand the membership for special meetings to get additional input or facilitate communications.

IMPLEMENTATION COMMITTEE

Employees are more supportive of change to the extent they understand and have an opportunity to influence the nature of the change. There is an adage that states "people support what they help to create." Implementation committees are frequently established to ensure that middle-level management, employees, and, if unionized, union stewards are involved and have the opportunity to influence the change.

Change efforts that have not involved middle management, either through committees or some other process, have experienced considerable resistance and poor implementation. Implementation committees consist of key middle-level managers and employees from the departments represented.

Implementation committees typically work closely with the steering committee.

Implementation Committee Role

The steering committee's role is planning and general direction. The implementation committee's is one of managing implementation on a day-to-day basis, which includes the following responsibilities:

- Establishing implementation plans and strategies.
- Determining training needs.
- Identifying factors that help or hinder the process, and taking corrective action.
- Stimulating upward communications, teamwork, and new approaches.
- Assuring that the following occur:
  - *a.* The change effort receives the support needed.
  - *b.* Input from the top and bottom are balanced.
  - *c.* Teams receive prompt answers to their recommendations or requests for information.
  - *d.* Teams receive help from the internal consultant or local facilitator, when needed.

Implementation Committee Membership

Typically, an implementation committee includes the following members:

1. Key managers responsible for large numbers of employees on whom change strategies will have an impact.
2. If the business is unionized, at least two union stewards.
3. Two employees who can provide a "reality test," because they are aware of employees's attitudes and opinions and are willing to speak up to provide dissonance.
4. Local internal consultant or facilitator.
5. All members should be perceived as competent in their present positions, and the committees should have no more than 10 members.

Unlike lower-level problem-solving teams, membership may not necessarily be voluntary, although members should be selected who want to participate. The reason participation is not totally voluntary for management and union officials is the same reason that other major changes in organization processes or direction are in most cases not voluntary.

When implementing a new budgeting or grievance procedure, people usually are not asked whether they want to volunteer to implement it. They should be given opportunities to influence how it is done. However, the decision to install a new procedure already has been made and management is expected to help implement the change.

The same is true for organizational change efforts. Middle managers and union stewards should have the opportunity to influence how they are implemented, but may not necessarily be given the opportunity to refute the decision by top management and union officials to proceed. In effect, the management of the organization has said it is looking for a new way to work together and managers and union stewards are asked to help find the way.

The decision for hourly employees to become involved is usually more voluntary, to avoid the change effort being a management dictate. Allowing employees the choice of whether to become involved in the early problem-solving teams clearly signals they will have an opportunity to influence what happens.

However, teams eventually may become a way of operating, as with the earlier General Foods's example. In that case, employees may not have the option to not be involved, as teams become the way the organization operates. Employees who are unable to participate on teams should be given other options within the organization. Some have chosen individual contributor roles while others, because of physical limitations, have assumed less than full rotation of jobs and have remained on jobs they could perform.

LINKAGE OF COMMITTEES

When several committees exist, communications and coordination are enhanced through overlapping membership. For example, having someone from the core group or the steering committee assigned as a member of or as a resource for implementation committees, and so forth, links the committees' communications and provides easy access from one committee to another to gain support and resources, or to resolve problems.

Whenever the following indicators appear, it is past time to get people together to talk about past actions and future plans.

- Frequent questions from top management about what is happening.
- Actions by top management that negatively affect the change effort. Sometimes directive decisions that are not explained or understood by the work force can be viewed as not moving in the direction of more team involvement.
- Questions from employees about the "why" or "what" of management actions.

The establishment of such structures as steering committees, implementation committees, and problem-solving teams signals to the organization that something is different and change is on the way. These are highly visible entities whose actions can be tracked and understood, and they provide a focus for responsibility for the change effort. If they function effectively and an esprit de corps develops within them, they help to energize the overall change effort. Having committee members from various parts of the organization provides a clear message that this is a total organization change and is not limited to one function or department.

COMMITTEE TEAMWORK

Developing an effective team and planning an effective participative effort require discussion and agreement on how the committee will function in five areas known as the "team hierarchy." Once higher-level committees understand how to manage themselves, they will be able to apply this model to other teams. The five areas represented in the hierarchy affect how a team functions and form the steps needed to build the steering committee into a team.

Early in their development, committees should meet for one to

FIGURE 6–4
Team Hierarchy

two days. The team hierarchy outlines the subjects for that meeting (see Figure 6–4). They should discuss the impact of outside factors on the committee, and agree on their goals, what the committee's role is, and the role of each member.[4] They should discuss improving the work processes, such as decision making, meetings, communicating, and building stronger working relationships.

SUMMARY

Team-based organizations either evolve from the existing structure or are newly designed. Both approaches use multi-level committees to involve those affected. The use of committees improves the design and increases employee commitment to success.

---

[4] James H. Shonk, *Working in Teams* (New York: Amacom, 1982). Now published by The Team Center, 21 Sarah Bishop Road, Ridgefield, Connecticut.

Chapter Seven

Designing a Team-Based Organization

A design team usually is created when an organization chooses to redesign the organization instead of starting with problem-solving teams and letting them evolve toward work teams with greater and greater autonomy. The design team is charged with conducting an analysis of the organization and recommending:

1. The design of jobs—that is, determining what tasks are included in a job.
2. The organization structure, including support, employee, and management functions.[1]
3. The number and composition of the teams.
4. Who and how others should be involved in the organization design and its implementation.

For example, the design team for a manufacturing facility was given the following charter:

---

[1] John J. Sherwood, *Creating Work Cultures with Competitive Advantage: Organizational Dynamics* (American Management Association, 1988), pp. 5–27.

DESIGN TEAM CHARTER

The vision of our future organization is one in which employee teams have the authority to manage their daily operations and participate in setting long-term direction and resource allocation. Our vision is guided by the following principles:

Teamwork

Teamwork is a way of life. Teams are multi-functional and self-supporting to the extent possible. All communications, actions, and decisions emphasize teamwork. Time and facilities are available to allow the team to function and make decisions at the lowest level.

Involvement

Each team is responsible for making the decisions to direct day-to-day operations and influence the end results of the business. The teams are trained in the skills and are provided the business information necessary to manage their operations and accomplish business objectives. The role of leadership is to provide overall direction and to coach and support the team.

Growth and Development

Personal and professional growth and development is encouraged. Individuals are given training and the opportunity to obtain skills and knowledge. Employees are rewarded for skill development and the use of multiple skills.

They were given this charter to design an organization with the following characteristics.

Characteristics of the Organization of the Future

1. • Multi-skilled employees.
   • Skill-based pay.
   • Rotating jobs among team.

2. • Multi-functional team based organization.
   • Teams self-managing and self-supporting to the extent possible.
3. The organization will have three levels, consisting of plant manager, team leader, and team member.
4. Other characteristics as determined by design team.

The role of the design team was as follows:

DESIGN TEAM ROLE

The role of the design team is to research, evaluate, and identify the ideal organization structure that will accomplish the vision.
   In fulfilling this role, the design team should:

• Identify but initially disregard the barriers and issues that will be faced in implementation.
• Keep communication open with the organization.
• Understand that their individual roles are to bring their knowledge and experience to the discussion.
• Make decisions collectively, by consensus, and in the best interest of the total organization.

The design team should specifically include in their consideration:

• What are the appropriate boundaries and makeup of the teams?
• What issues should be addressed consistently across the teams?
• Determine what future design teams should be formed and what their role should be.
• Identify issues to be forwarded to future mini-design teams. Mini-design teams are composed of employees in the area being redesigned. They work out the details of implementing the new organization.

DESIGN TEAM MEMBERSHIP

Membership should be limited to keep the team at a workable size, preferably no more than 11. To ensure the team has the expertise needed, members are selected who represent all levels and major departments within the organization. Sometimes members are selected by the core group. In other cases, employees can volunteer for a selection team that selects among the volunteers in their department.

SEQUENCE OF TASKS

The specific tasks that design teams typically undertake to research, evaluate, and identify the ideal organization structure are outlined in the following diagram (see Figure 7–1). The process is not as linear as depicted. There are frequent feedback loops and constant recycling of information.

FIGURE 7–1
Design Team Tasks

Analyze the technical system and determine the implications for organization structure and work processes.

↓

Determine the preliminary major boundaries by using technical system analysis and boundary determinants.

↓

Determine jobs and teams by using technical system analysis, social system analysis, and boundary determinants.

↓

Determine final organizational boundaries, including business units, teams, and jobs.

ANALYSIS OF TECHNICAL SYSTEM

The first activity of a design team is to analyze the technical system to understand how work flows through the organization and to determine where variances occur from expected outcomes. The following seven steps in a technical analysis are adapted from work done by Hanna, who presents a very workable level of detail for designing an organization.[2]

The newly designed organization structure should reflect the findings of this analysis and, to the extent possible, correct the variances that presently occur.

1. Identify the major steps of the work process, tracing the flow of material and information from start to finish. This involves listing each step in the process of producing the product, such as the receiving of raw material, mixing raw materials, processing, packaging, and shipping.

2. Identify variances in the product or service from expected results. A variance is any other thing that happens than an expected result. For example, in making paper it could be holes in the paper or incorrect color.

3. Identify where the variances are first observed. This is the place in the process where someone first notices that the product is not as expected.

4. Identify where the variances are controlled or corrected and by whom. This is the point in the process where someone corrects the problem—for example, changes the color. Frequently, the person who can control the variance is not the person who first sees it. It is noticed downstream from where the problem occurs and is eventually corrected. Therefore, communication between the two individuals is needed to correct the variance earlier or where it occurs.

---

[2] David P. Hanna, *Designing Organizations for High Performance* (Reading, Mass.: Addison Wesley Publishing, 1988).

5. Identify the tasks that need to be performed to correct the variances. This involves identifying all the tasks or actions required by the operator of the equipment, the maintenance personnel, and the others to correct the problem. Sometimes it is a simple adjustment to the machine or a change of raw material stock, or it can involve complex machine repair.

6. Identify the knowledge and skills that are required to perform the tasks to correct the variances—preferably before they occur. The intent is to give employees the information and skills required to prevent the variance.

7. Determine what information and cooperation or teamwork are needed to effectively perform the work. Also, identify who has to coordinate with whom to identify and correct the problems.

Doing the analysis is only the beginning. Now the design team must determine the implications of this analysis. The members should review their data and determine the implications for the following:

• Correcting variances where they occur or closer to where they occur. The purpose is to identify and correct the problem where or before it happens.

• Changes in work processes to reduce or eliminate variances. Can something be changed in the work flow, such as how raw materials are mixed, that will correct the problem or reduce the number of variances?

• Information or training required to give people the multiple knowledge and skills needed to control or correct variances before they happen. If employees have a broad understanding of the manufacturing process, they are better able to identify why problems occur and determine how to correct them.

• Cooperation or teamwork needed to perform the work effectively. The purpose of this step is to identify where closer coordination of employees' efforts would result in a better product or service. To illustrate, the person adding color to the paper perhaps should work more closely with the person running the paper machine to ensure they are getting the right color immediately, rather than after they have produced a large quantity of off-color product.

• Either increased teamwork or changes in organization structure to put people who should be working closer together on the same team. In one organization, to reduce the amount of damage to finished goods and better control the supply of raw materials, truck lift drivers who supplied materials and carted away finished goods were put on the same team as those manufacturing the product.

• Changes in systems—for example, communications or procedures. Sometimes getting more timely information can greatly reduce variances.

Test of Re-design Against Analysis of Technical System

The following questions can be used by the design team once the members have decided how the organization should change, based on the technical analysis. Each member should complete the questionnaire and then discuss his or her answers in a team meeting. Such a test can serve to identify additional changes but equally important it can reaffirm that the recommendations are on target.

1. Does the redesign correct variances where they occur?

_____

_____

   A. Identify the variances.

_____

_____

   B. Compare where variances are controlled in the new design versus the present organization.

_____

_____

C. Are there any changes necessary in the new design to better control variances?

_____

_____

2. Do employees have the knowledge or skill needed to correct variances where they occur?

_____

_____

A. What additional knowledge or skill is needed?

_____

_____

B. What training is needed?

_____

_____

3. Does the new organization put people together who will need to communicate and coordinate their activities to effectively perform their work and correct variances?

_____

_____

A. Are people who need to communicate and coordinate on the same teams?

_____

_____

B. What, if any, changes in team membership are indicated?

_____

_____

4. Does the new organization require any changes in systems, procedures, or communications for teams to function effectively and correct variances?

_____

_____

A. Systems changes.

_____

_____

B. Procedures changes.

_____

_____

C. Communications changes.

_____

_____

- Additional information needed by team.

_____

_____

BOUNDARY DETERMINANTS

On completing the technical analysis and identifying the implications, the next step for the design team is to determine the major organizational boundaries—for example, departments or business units. Keep in mind that this is not a cookbook and, therefore, do whatever works for you.

Boundary determinants are guidelines used to identify self-sufficient business units and teams divided according to natural boundaries related to the work. Many of the items listed below are adapted from Hanna's book on designing organizations.[3] Purposely, no weight is given to the boundary determinants. Each organization must decide what is most important to their success. There are trade-offs that will need to be made, based on the existing technology, size of facility, and the likes.

1. Technical analysis.
The findings of the technical analysis are used to determine implications for the optimum organization structure and work processes. It usually helps to determine what people or departments need to work closely together to reduce variances. This leads to a determination of whether new configurations different than the existing departments are needed.

2. Product form change.
Natural breaks in the process will provide clues for identifying the self-sufficient subsystems. These breaks occur where there is a change in the state of the product—for example, a change in form or additional materials added.

In one organization, the manufacturing business team makes a huge roll of paper, weighing several hundreds of pounds. The second team cuts the paper into strips and sheets and boxes it. The product clearly changes form from one team to the other, and a very different technology is required for each process. They have two separate business units doing these tasks.

3. Technology.
Technology may be so complex or differentiated that no individual or team can handle all operations. If so, departmentalization may be needed. In the above example, different technologies were required, which led to the creation of two different business

---

[3] Ibid.

units, each with several teams. The knowledge required to function as a member of a team and rotate among several tasks was too great to combine the two units into one.

4. Territory.
A building's layout or the geography covered may make physical proximity throughout the entire process an impossibility; if so, departmentalization might be required. To illustrate, sales forces tend to be divided by region or district. Long assembly lines that wind throughout one or several buildings may be departmentalized and consist of several subteams. Customer service teams sometimes are assigned a territory.

5. Time.
Time may become a basis for segmenting work when the task exceeds the allotted time for an individual or team to complete it—for example, in continuous production processes, shifts divide the task into manageable bits. Long-term/short-term orientation also can be a factor in segmenting work—for example, long-term research versus short-term product service or development.

6. Interdependence.
Work units should minimize the need to reach across organizational boundaries for the resources to complete their work. Resources should be inside the department where they are regularly used. There may be areas where the economies of scale or the use of scarce resources might dictate centralizing the resource.

To give an example, it may be more feasible economically to do all purchasing by one department or to centralize scarce or infrequently used skills, so they can be applied throughout the organization. Conversely, minor maintenance may be better handled within a production team versus supplied from an outside maintenance team.

7. Size.
The optimal size of a team ranges from 3 to 14 members. Even teams of 14 will find it difficult to make decisions, maintain physical proximity, and share the work effectively.

8. Client.
Sometimes teams are organized around a client they service. The team is responsible for client contacts and services. A major credit

card firm is putting together teams to so handle certain clients that, when customers call, each person can answer their questions instead of transferring the customer or putting them on hold for long periods.

A client focus also limits the scope of knowledge needed to cover a larger number of clients. This focus also allows employees to have a more in-depth knowledge of the client's needs and to handle most of the operations required.

ANALYSIS OF SOCIAL SYSTEM

The boundary determinants should help in deciding on the major business units and in determining the teams within them. Next, the analysis of the social system helps to further define the jobs within the teams and whether they are satisfying and meaningful. Several criteria can be used. I have found a combination of Trist's and Hackman's variables to be most useful.[4,5] The following criteria are used to structure teams and jobs for optimum employee commitment and job satisfaction—the prime prerequisites to high performance.

1. Information.
Employees get adequate *information* and *feedback* of results to operate autonomously. Not knowing that you are producing junk doesn't allow you to correct the problem. When one team learned how much the company was losing by discarding the large tubes that raw material came on, the members devised a plan to recycle and thus lowered their costs considerably.

2. Challenging job.
The job is reasonably demanding, other than sheer endurance. Jobs require a variety of skills and talents. Performing one task all

[4] E. A. Trist, "Socio-Technical Critique of Scientific Management," a paper contributed to the Edinburgh Conference on the Impact of Science and Technology, Edinburgh University, May 24–26, 1970.

[5] J. Richard Hackman and Seig R. Oldham, *Work Redesign* (Reading, Mass.: Addison Wesley Publishing, 1980), pp. 77–80.

day can be repetitive and doesn't challenge one's ability. Some workers may prefer this type of work. However, many may become bored.

3. Decision-making autonomy.

The job provides decision-making freedom—for example, scheduling the work, deciding how to do the work, and correcting variances.

4. Whole job.

The job requires completion of a whole task—an identifiable piece of work. Also, doing a job from beginning to end with a visible outcome. Assemblers of small electronic devices, such as pagers, have gone from employees doing one task, such as soldering the same piece over and over, to either a complete or a subassembly of the product, depending on the complexity of the task.

5. Job significance.

The job makes a contribution to the utility of the product or has a substantial impact on the lives or work of others within or outside the organization.

6. Teamwork.

Providing opportunities for social support and interaction with others.

Three criteria for grouping individual jobs into teams are:

- Employees have a common goal and are interdependent— that is, they must coordinate their activities to accomplish the goal.
- There is a relatively high level of stress in individual tasks, and team support or job rotation will reduce the stress.
- Individual jobs do not make an obvious perceivable contribution to the end product. By combining that job into the total team's responsibility, individuals who had performed that job can now take on other team responsibilities and rotate through the job.

The amount of time required for design teams to be educated and develop a recommendation varies, depending on the size and complexity of the organization. Generally, it takes months and not days. The final organization structure, to the extent possible, should optimize the results of the technical and social analysis and the boundary determinants. It may be the result of many trade-offs between the many factors considered. Ultimately, there should be a logical congruence to the organization—that is, all the pieces should fit together.

Analysis of Social System Questionnaire

The following questions are to help the design team decide how the social system should change. Answering the questions will help to determine whether the jobs that make up a team are satisfying and meaningful. The questions are built around Hackman and Trist's criteria for structuring teams and jobs for optimum employee commitment, job satisfaction, and organizational performance.

To obtain the largest number of ideas, it is usually best to have each design team member individually answer the questions and then have a team discussion to agree on the best solutions.

1. **Information.**
   Employees get adequate *information* and *feedback* of results to operate autonomously.

   A. What information will employees need to perform autonomously?

   _____

   B. How will they get the needed information in the new organization?

   _____

   _____

2. **Challenging job.**
   The job is reasonably demanding, other than sheer endurance. Jobs require a variety of skills and talents.

   A. Is a variety of skills required for each job? If not, will employees rotate through the job hourly or daily?

_____

_____

B. Is a variety of skills required on each team?

_____

_____

C. Will employees on the teams be able to learn new skills?

_____

_____

D. How long will it take to learn all the skills? Is this too short or too long a time?

_____

_____

3. **Decision making/autonomy.**
   The job provides freedom, such as scheduling the work and deciding how to do the work and correct variances.

   A. Do all jobs contain some decision-making authority?

   _____

   _____

   B. Do teams have the decision-making authority needed to control variances and accomplish their work?

   _____

   _____

C. Are there decisions in the new organization where it is unclear who will make them?

_____

_____

4. Whole job.
The job requires completion of a whole task—an identifiable piece of work—doing a job from beginning to end with a visible outcome.

A. Are there any jobs where employees will be doing a very small piece of an overall task?

_____

_____

B. Will there be visible outcomes of each job?

_____

_____

5. Job significance.
The job makes a contribution to the utility of the product or has a substantial impact on the lives or work of others within or outside of the organization.

A. Will employees feel that their job is significant/important to the overall operation?

_____

_____

B. Do all jobs add to the utility of the product?

_____

_____

6. **Teamwork.**
   Individual jobs should be grouped into teams when:
   - Employees have a common goal and are interdependent—that is, they must coordinate their activities.
   - There is a relatively high level of stress in individual tasks.
   - Individual jobs do not make an obvious perceivable contribution to the end product.

   A. Are the jobs that are grouped into a team interdependent—that is, do they require team members to coordinate to accomplish the team task?

   _____

   _____

   B. Are stressful jobs part of a team and will people frequently rotate through those jobs?

   _____

   _____

   C. Have jobs that do not make a perceivable contribution to the end product been incorporated into a team?

   _____

   _____

   D. Where will cross-team or business unit teamwork be needed?

   _____

   _____

   E. How will shifts communicate with each other?

   _____

   _____

PLANNING FOR TEAMS

The following questions are intended to help the planners of change—usually a design team or core group—ensure that the new organization will support teams. It addresses many of the issues identified in the teamwork foundation. After answering the questions, the planning group should develop appropriate actions.

Management Philosophy

1. Do we have an explicit or implicit high involvement management philosophy?
2. Do we take a long-term approach to managing the business and developing people?
3. What actions are needed regarding philosophy?
   By whom?
   Actions:
   Persons responsible:
   Timing:

Organization Structure

1. How many levels of management are needed to most effectively manage our business?
2. What are the levels and their responsibility and authority?
3. What changes are required to make this new organization work—for example:
   Decision-making authority?
   Information availability?
   Actions:
   Persons responsible:
   Timing:

Rewards

1. Does our reward system support our core values, e.g. organization effectiveness, employee commitment, self-management, personal and career growth, and flexibility?
2. Are the present psychological and monetary rewards supportive of the type of organization we are trying to create?
3. Do we reward teams and teamwork—through either "pay for knowledge" or a team reward system?
   Actions:
   Persons responsible:
   Timing:

Information

1. What information will employees need to self-manage and make effective decisions?
2. What systems are needed to give them this information?
   Actions:
   Persons responsible:
   Timing:

Employment Stability

1. What can be done to stabilize employment?
   Actions:
   Persons responsible:
   Timing:

Equal Treatment

1. What can be done to reduce status differences and make everyone feel each is a part of the team?

2. Do our policies and practices treat people equally?
   Actions:
   Persons responsible:
   Timing:

Decision Making

1. Do jobs provide employees with the authority and information they need? .
   Actions:
   Persons responsible:
   Timing:

Skills

1. What skills will be required to effectively work in this organization?
   Actions:
   Persons responsible:
   Timing:

CORE GROUP ROLE

A core group usually determines the design team's charter and approves the team's final recommendations. The core group's approval helps to ensure that the recommendations fit with the charter and that any identified organizational constraints are met.

The core group should be careful not to cut off ideas too quickly; rather, it should allow the design team to fully explore organizational design options and test them against the charter. A close working relationship should be maintained between the two groups, with frequent meetings to inform the core group on the progress of the design team.

The design team also should be responsible for making recommendations on how to implement the new design. However, the ultimate responsibility for implementation usually rests with line management. They are the ones who must support and nurture the new organization.

The implementation of the new team-based organization is gradual. Teams take on the responsibilities they can easily assume, either because they require less training or because the team members already do the tasks when the supervisor is out. Depending upon the speed of implementation, the new design approach may not look much different from the evolution approach, because, usually, teams gradually assume more autonomy.

SUMMARY

The design team is charged with recommending how to structure teams in a way that optimizes the social and technical systems. With agreement by the core group of the design team's recommendations, the next step usually is to inform employees and begin building the skills to implement the new organization. Chapter Eight will outline the steps and programs involved in training employees and managers to work in teams.

Chapter Eight
Training

Organizations are in favor of training but frequently can't find the time to do it. There is usually time to train managers, but it is difficult to train employees. Training is difficult to schedule, especially in continuous process operations, and is costly. Although scheduling is difficult and time off the job is costly, the training of managers and teams will provide that extra boost needed to launch a team-based organization.

Organizations that skipped the training or over time let it lapse have had to go back and train, to correct difficulties with their teams. You can implement teams without training but there is a cost. Without training, teams are slow to mature and some may never reach a productive working level. Unproductive work habits may develop and team members may become disillusioned with each other and their ability to function effectively.

For example, a review of the experience of a production team that was made autonomous overnight without training illustrates these problems. The team had the benefit of a leader/coach for the first year but no training. After working together for three years, management and the team felt they had not jelled and could be doing better and enjoying work more. Interviews with the team members showed the following:

- They felt their meetings were unproductive.
- There was considerable conflict on the team.
- They felt alienated from management. Their team leader/ coach left after one year, and they had had a series of managers whose roles had not been well-defined.
- The team coordinator's role was ill-defined and underused. The team coordinator position rotated among the team's members on a monthly basis.
- There were few agreed-to teamwork guidelines and very different expectations among team members about how the team should function.
- When asked if they liked working as a self-directed team versus the previous traditional way of working, they all said emphatically and unequivocally that they preferred working in a team.
- Despite these problems the team had shown significant increases in productivity over the previous way of working.

As a result of the interviews, the team went through a two-day team-training/team-building program. During this program, the team was trained in basic listening and communications skills, conducting meetings, and conflict resolution. With the help of the trainers, the team then conducted its own meeting and addressed the issues of management alienation, the coordinator's role, working guidelines, and norms of behavior and conflicts among team members.

The overwhelming feedback by the team and the department manager was that they should have had this training when they started. Several weeks after the training, the feedback from the team and the manager was that their problems were being addressed and resolved. They agreed to meet regularly to plan and address problems.

A few months after the training, the team proudly posted a letter on the bulletin board showing its improvement in safety, quality, and production over a three-year period. The team ended the letter with this:

We have come a long way and there is no limit to hold us down. We, as a team, feel good about ourselves, the business, and the company; and the future belongs to us. We will be the best in the business because we believe in ourselves and teams.

The training to support a move toward a team-based organization will differ somewhat by the organization, depending upon the organization's training history and change strategy. However, generic types of training have been used by many organizations. The training program's chart identifies seven generic types of training and lists their purpose, participants, and content (see Figure 8–1).

Calling the items on the chart "training programs" does not capture what many of them are. Training typically conjures an image of knowledge and skill building and practice. In addition to this, many of the programs listed engage the participants in planning and problem solving. They address the issues facing them as either a planning or a work team.

START-UP

A large number of change efforts start with training, because it can be very helpful to build needed knowledge and understanding. The first session—the start-up workshop—as described in the list of training programs, is designed to expose top management to what a team-based organization is, what other companies are doing, and the concepts underlying how to change to a fuller use of teams.

This same program, or one of similar content, is then frequently conducted for other levels of management within the organization. The core group usually goes through start-up training first. At the conclusion, the group develops plans for educating others and starting the change effort.

FIGURE 8–1
Training Programs

Program/Audience/Purpose	Content
1. Start-up Core group members Steering committee members Design team members **Purpose:** Build knowledge and understanding of how team-based organizations work, what is required to make the change, and how they can benefit the organization.	Identifying goals. Clarifying roles: committees, management, union employees. Building committee teamwork. Learning how to build teams. Socio-technical systems. Team leadership. Planning, developing, and implementing change.
2. Trips to other companies **Purpose:** See firsthand how team-based organizations work and the process of implementing them.	Tour of work areas. Discussion with managers, union officers, and employees.
3. Coordinator Coordinators Meeting facilitators **Purpose:** Build internal team facilitation and consulting skills.	Consulting and group facilitation skills. Consultant's/facilitator's role. Understanding and consulting with teams. Conducting effective meetings. Resolving conflict. Understanding and facilitating change.
4. Team leader Team leaders **Purpose:** Develop team leadership skills.	How to work in and build teams. Leading participative meetings. Role of the leader.
5. Orientations Employees **Purpose:** Build understanding of team-based organizations, how they impact upon employees, and how to get involved.	What is a team-based organization. How the changes will affect employees. How to participate.
6. Teamwork Members of team, including leader **Purpose:** Develop the ability of the team to work together.	How to work in teams/team building. Team meetings. Conflict-resolution skills. Interpersonal skills.

FIGURE 8–1 (*continued*)

Program/Audience/Purpose	Content
7. Job skills Members of self-managing teams **Purpose:** Teach new technical skills required of team members.	Specific job skills required to function on a self-managing team.

TRIPS TO OTHER COMPANIES

The start-up training frequently is followed by trips to other companies to see firsthand how they organize and use teams. It can be very helpful to talk with managers of other companies who have installed team-based organizations. The information gained during these trips is frequently quite detailed and greatly increases your understanding of how to utilize teams in your organization.

The trips can be a very effective mechanism for middle managers, employees, and union officers to learn more about teams as well as to increase their acceptance of teams as a possible approach to improving the effectiveness of the organization. Seminars conducted by local universities, consultants, and organizations—like the Organization Development Network—can be very helpful in providing managers with information about what other companies are doing.

COORDINATOR

Once top management and—if it is a joint effort—the union have decided they want to move ahead with their team-based change effort, the next step, typically, is to build internal expertise.

Depending on the nature of the change effort and the size of the organization, some businesses have chosen to create coordinators—often people in human resources positions—who can spread the ideas to the various outlying locations, offices, factories, and the like. Other organizations have chosen to build the facilitation skills within the leadership ranks and have trained supervisors to provide the facilitating skills.

A major credit company with well over 100 branch offices throughout the United States has used both strategies. Its internal training staff worked with outside consultants to develop and deliver training to managers. The managers were trained to launch and facilitate team efforts, and the internal training staff became consultants to the managers. This was the only way the training staff felt they could help the large number of branches and maintain the local leadership that they felt was necessary to make the change to teams successful in each branch.

The coordinator's workshop is designed to train internal coordinators to work with managers and teams and thus help them implement the desired change. Sometimes internal coordinators are selected and trained prior to steering committee start-up, so these people can attend and help facilitate the steering committee meetings and go through training with the committee. Frequently, organizations rely heavily on outside resources to help them launch a team-based change effort and train the internal resources by having them work alongside the consultant. It is the internal resources who will be called upon to maintain this effort once the outside consultants have gone, and they will need team-building and team-facilitation skills.

TEAM LEADER

The fourth item on the list of training programs is team-leader training. The purpose of this training is to teach team leaders how to work with teams, and how it differs or is similar to their past ways of leading. A team leader's role is to be a coach. He or she is trained to lead teams, through the use of facilitating and coaching skills.

Another purpose of this training can be to address team leaders' concerns about how well they will do in their new role and how much support they will receive from their managers. A team leader's manager also should attend this program to build understanding and a support relationship between them.

The experience with team-leader training to date leads me to believe it needs to be continually reinforced with short training sessions and with opportunities for team leaders to exchange ideas. A major corporation has monthly team-leader meetings, where the leaders can exchange ideas, make recommendations for change, and receive help and support from their managers on issues of concern.

Team leaders and coordinators are frequently used in conducting the employee orientations and team training. This puts them in the training/coaching role and helps employees see how to use their expertise and knowledge of teams.

ORIENTATIONS

At some point in the process, employees need to be aware of what is being planned, the impact that these changes will have on them, and how they can get involved. This usually is done through employee orientations. If it is a joint management/union effort, these orientations can be especially important for the union, because they provide a communications vehicle and a way for the union to help gain employee support for the changes.

Frequently, there is more than one orientation. First comes an announcement that the organization is undertaking and planning a change toward greater utilization of teams. After the design and steering committees have worked for some time, there may be additional orientations to inform the employees on the progress to date and to answer questions. Finally, there will be an orientation to tell employees what has been developed, how it will impact upon them, how they can get involved, and answer any concerns they have.

These orientations should not be considered a replacement for some form of daily feedback to employees about what is being planned that provides them an opportunity to input into those plans and influence the final outcomes. In one organization, the design team, on a weekly basis, kept the members of the organization informed of its plans. The net result was a high level of understanding of future plans and considerable discussion and altering of issues to address people's concerns as they arose. Whereas, in another organization that did not have frequent updates, the announcement of the "final plan" met with considerable uproar and resistance.

TEAMWORK

Team training gets teams off to a faster start—that is, accelerates their ability to function as an effective team. The training also reduces the likelihood of teams having early failure experiences. This training usually emphasizes teamwork and the ability of the members to work together in a participative manner to solve problems and make decisions.

The program for teams called "Teamwork" emphasizes building an understanding of the essential skills and knowledge for an effective team. Team members have an opportunity to practice these skills during the program.

Learning is facilitated by teams exploring together and determining what is most appropriate for them in terms of how they should meet, communicate, and make decisions. While the team is learning the skills and knowledge necessary for effective teamwork, it also begins to apply them by working on real issues. They also plan how the team will work in the future. The program is attended by the entire team. It is not merely training, it is a highly involving step toward improving their ability to work together.

Depending on the focus of the Teamwork program, the outcomes might be an improvement of the team's ability to function collaboratively; a clear identification of the team's goals and priorities; a clarification and understanding of each team member's roles; identification of the decision-making communications and meetings processes required by the team to operate effectively; identification of and a plan to deal with forces that might impact on the team's performance from the larger organization; and a work plan for the team on what it will be asked to do over the next few months.

One organization starts up its teams by having them attend a three-day Teamwork program. During this program they have consistently experienced a group of workers being transformed into a team that can conduct team meetings, listen to all members' points of view, and make consensus decisions.

The culmination of the training has been the nomination and selection of the team's first rotating team leader. During the selection process, nominees present why they want the job and then wait outside the meeting room while the team discusses each candidate's merits—not flaws—and selects its first team leader.

Selecting a leader and discussing the merits of one's peers are typically very difficult issues for teams to deal with, even after working together for a long time. I believe the trust built during the training and the acquisition of team problem-solving and communications skills greatly contributes to their ability to choose a leader.

JOB SKILLS

Employees may need to learn new or multiple job skills as a result of the organization redesign. For example, if employees rotate jobs, they may need to learn several jobs. Much of the training of these new skills is on-the-job training or programs that usually are developed by the internal training staff.

MIXING LEVELS

Sometimes it is helpful to have a mixture of management, union, and employees in training programs. This provides a balanced point of view, relative to how the organization is presently functioning—compared to the future charter. An important aspect of much of the training is the examination of the current level of participation and teamwork within the organization, relative to the desired amount. By having a balanced view from all levels of the organization, it encourages a richer discussion of options for the future.

During the initial diagnosis to determine how participative an organization is, we typically find that the higher up the training goes in the levels of management, the higher the rating that is given to the organization on participation and teamwork. Putting several levels together during training encourages multiple points of view and much richer discussion and problem-solving.

TIMING

Training should occur just prior to the time when participants have to apply the concepts and skills being taught. This provides an immediate opportunity to use the knowledge gained and to practice the skills learned.

In one organization, management complained about the lack of supervisors applying the training they were given over the years. A closer examination revealed that, after the training, supervisors were not required to use different skills. In fact, the organization had not launched any type of change effort that would lead to supervisors behaving differently. The result was that the newly learned skills soon atrophied or supervisors did not see an opportunity to apply them in the old "traditionally operated" organization.

By placing training close to the time that skills are to be applied, you increase the transfer of knowledge and skill. It also makes training an event that signals to the organization something new or different is about to happen. Managers and employees tend to respond, to get involved in events, and to see them as significant points in time when change should occur.

MAKING LEARNING A WAY OF LIFE

Training is not a one-shot experience. New employees will be hired and will require the training received by the existing staff.

A greenfield manufacturing facility had been operating very successfully for three years. It had done significant up-front training. During a visit to this facility, a manager related to me that the facility had not done much training since the start-up and, as a result, were beginning to feel some repercussions. The manager found that newly hired employees were not picking up the skills by being in teams as had been hoped. Also teams were beginning to develop sloppy habits and that a training refresher would be helpful.

Management and employee committees should be charged with the responsibility of periodically examining what additional training will be helpful to the organization. In addition, as new and better ways of operating are discovered, a method should be developed to disseminate throughout the organization what has been learned. For example, team leaders in one organization meet regularly to share what they have learned and to have a dialogue with top management about how new ideas can be implemented throughout the organization.

The lack of feedback and learning can be fatal to an organization change effort. I was asked by the management to help rejuvenate a "failing" team-based change effort.

The first step was to interview managers and employees to determine why the effort was failing. The consistent feedback from management was that employees don't care. "They aren't taking being a team seriously." Employees said that management wasn't serious about teams. Further probing revealed that teams started well but at the point where teams wanted to take on more responsibility, they felt that managers were resisting. The result was employees saying "you see I knew they weren't serious."

This organization had not set up an effective method to get two-way feedback and learn from it and adapt accordingly. As the team effort matures, teams will increase in capability and desired responsibility. This will require changes in management's and the team's behavior. As the organization environment changes, so must the organization and teams respond in whatever ways are appropriate. Continual learning and adaptation are essential for success.

SUMMARY

Operating an effective team-based organization requires that people have the necessary skills. Teams are not a quick fix for an organization's problems. The teams require training and continuous learning as they adapt to the environmental challenges.

Chapter Nine
Leading a Team-Based Organization

Team-based organizations require leadership. Leading the teams is similar to coaching. It involves assessing the teams' skills and helping them use them to the fullest. Employees tend to more effectively contribute when they are coached to make optimal use of their strengths and resources. Managers should stimulate the process of increased employee initiative and autonomy by providing general direction, contributing their own ideas, helping to identify alternatives, raising questions, and supplying informational feedback. The managers' role becomes one of helping others to define, analyze, and solve problems.

Leading a participative team requires that the manager solicit considerably more input into decisions, share decision-making responsibility, or delegate specifically identified decisions to the team. Decisions, once given the appropriate information and training, the team can make.

Managers not accustomed to leading in this manner frequently fear that it means giving all their authority to employees. In fact, the process of delegating more authority to teams is usually gradual and based on the team's abilities. How rapidly a manager delegates to a team depends on the level of employee knowledge, training, and willingness to take on more of the daily management of work.

Until managers develop an understanding of how the leading of teams is different than the managing of individuals, they may feel anxious. While their role is evolving, managers need to be assured that their jobs will not disappear—and that their new job can be rewarding and productive.

One organization, faced with the reduction of management levels and, specifically, the elimination of the first line supervisor's role, assured supervisors that it would maintain their pay and that it would help them prepare for the job of team coach, as long as they were willing and capable, or find them another position.

Although the team leaders do not make many of the decisions they had made in the past or solve problems, they are responsible for seeing that decisions are made and problems solved. Teams mean extensive participation by employees in areas traditionally reserved for management, but the participation does not mean an abdication of management's responsibility for results. Teams and managers share this responsibility. When employees are given the opportunity to contribute more actively and accept increased responsibility, the positive changes they generate will reflect well on the leader.

The team leader's role is to see that the best decisions and plans are made and supported. Decisions made with little involvement from those who have to implement them often meet with resistance, because the implementer either doesn't understand or agree. Therefore, as leaders seek more input, which takes more time, the ultimate plan or decision is based on more information and employee participation and so receives greater acceptance.

Over time, the supervisor's role evolves from one of monitoring and directing the team to one of facilitating the work of the team and managing their interface with the rest of the organization.[1]

Tannenbaum and Schmidt have described how the decision-making responsibilities of managers change in terms of a contin-

---

[1]William B. Werther, "Productivity Improvement through People," *Arizona Business*, February 1981, pp. 15–16.

uum, in which the manager exerts nearly all of the influence on one end of the continuum and employees exert most of the influence on the other.[2] Bramlette describes an evolution in management's role from one-on-one decision maker to team leader to boundary manager.[3]

ONE-ON-ONE MANAGER

As the role implies, one-on-one managers work individually with people. Typically, they make the decisions with input from individuals. However, one-on-one management can be very participative.

The one-on-one supervisor holds few meetings. Meetings are mostly for disseminating information.

TEAM LEADER

The team leader thinks in terms of managing a team that needs to accomplish an overall task, as opposed to individuals who must do a particular piece of work. In addition to thinking about employees as individuals, the team leader also is concerned about the performance of the team.

The team leader helps to so organize the team that it can operate in a productive manner. The role is to enable others to function effectively. Decisions are shared with the team and, typically, are made by consensus. Group members have the responsibility for identifying issues and resolving them.

The team leader serves as a discussion leader during team meetings. The leader's attention shifts from making decisions to making sure the appropriate issues are addressed and good decisions are made. Team members help set meeting agendas, make decisions, and identify follow-up responsibilities.

---

[2]Robert Tannenbaum and Warren Schmidt, "How to Choose a Leadership Pattern," *Harvard Business Review* 36, March–April 1958, pp. 95–101.

[3]Carl A. Bramlette, *Free to Change* (Washington, D.C.: American Society for Training and Development, 1984).

The team leader's role as a coach is to gain team members' commitment and find ways to best employ their talents. To do this requires good group facilitation skills, such as keeping the discussion open while moving toward a solution.

Since greater emphasis is on personal and team commitment, the use of total management authority diminishes. It is supplanted by an attitude of trust, confidence, and respect. Team-leader behavior can range from the leader being in control to giving the team high autonomy. Both modes may be appropriate, depending on the issue, time constraints, and maturity of the team.

TEAM BOUNDARY MANAGER

The team boundary manager manages the interaction of the team with its environment. The day-to-day running of the operation is delegated to the team. Since the majority of the operating decisions have been delegated to the team, the boundary manager works at providing quality information, so the team can make informed choices. The boundary manager manages the interface with other teams, so the work flows smoothly between them and helps acquire needed resources.

Meetings are the responsibility of the team. The boundary manager is a resource; he or she provides input on key interface and resource allocation issues.

TEAM LEADERSHIP CONTINUUM

The team leadership continuum illustrates the different behaviors of a one-on-one manager, a team leader, and a boundary manager. Leading teams, rather than managing individuals, requires operating more as a team leader or boundary manager, as outlined in the following chart. This does not mean that one-on-one contact is not needed from time to time—for example, for employee counseling or training.

Team Leadership Continuum

**Individual-centered
Leadership**

**Team-centered
Leadership**

| Low--------------------- Team Autonomy--------------------- High |

One-on-one Manager	*Team Leader*	*Team Boundary Manager*
1	*2*	*3*

1. Goal setting.

1	*2*	*3*
Manager sets individual goals with each individual.	Team with leader sets team goals.	Team sets team goals. Manager ensures fit with larger organization.

2. Planning.

1	*2*	*3*
Manager plans, reviews, and gets input.	Team plans with leader.	Team plans. Manager coordinates plans with other units.

3. Organization Structure.

1	*2*	*3*
Hierarchy, with clear chain of command.	Flat structure; leader part of team.	Flat structure; leader manages boundary and is a resource to team.

4. Roles.

1	2	3
Clearly defined management and employee responsibility.	Shared responsibility. Leader provides some direction and facilitates teamwork.	Team has responsibility within defined limits. Leader manages boundary and is a resource to the team.

5. Decision making.

1	2	3
Manager gets input and decides.	Team and leader decide; consensus.	Team decides within defined limits.

6. Meeting.

1	2	3
Frequently one on one. Manager sets agenda. Manager leads.	Team and leader jointly set agenda and meet. Team leader leads.	Team sets agenda and meets without boundary manager. Leadership rotates. Manager is a resource.

7. Communications.

1	2	3
Mostly one on one and frequently dependent upon manager.	Team responsibility. All team members and leader in the communications loop.	Team keeps boundary manager informed. Manager communicates with groups outside the team.

8. Control.

1	2	3
Manager and individual exercise control.	Team and leader exercise control.	Team exercises control. Boundary manager kept informed.

9. Performance feedback.

1	2	3
Manager and individual assess individual's performance.	Team and leader assess team's performance.	Team assesses team's performance. Boundary manager provides input.

ANALYZING YOUR LEADERSHIP

To assess how you are managing teams, review the nine items on the Team Leadership Continuum and circle the number that best describes your overall approach. Recognize, however, that all are appropriate, depending upon the situation. After analyzing your leadership approach, answer the following questions:

- Does my approach fully use the talents of the team?
- Does my approach build team commitment?
- What approach do team members prefer for the most effective team?
- How should I alter my approach to leading teams?

INTERFACE WITH LARGER SYSTEM

Another important management responsibility is managing the interface between the changing unit and the larger system. Walton describes the problems of being the innovative part of an organization and how the innovative unit encounters many obstacles, including bureaucratic red tape.[4]

For instance, simple decisions may become major issues, such as who selects the new controller for an operating unit. In one organization, tradition dictated that the corporate controller's office make the selection. However, local management wanted to make the decision to ensure selection of someone supportive of the newly established management style.

In another example, the innovative unit told corporate management that, because of lean staffing, the unit no longer could answer all the requests for financial data and certainly not as rapidly as had been done in the past.

In summary, successful changes at the operating unit frequently require a concomitant change in the larger system, or at least some experimental protection.

The parts of the organization undergoing change develop an understanding of what is needed to support long-lasting change more rapidly than those further removed from the changes. Those not as directly involved tend to have less of a first hand understanding of the extent and nature of organizational change required to support teams.

A common example of this is the perception by corporate managers that the present compensation system will accommodate teams. The area changing to a greater use of teams frequently wants to alter the compensation system to better reward the teams. Consequently, the changing unit frequently is placed in the position of requesting organizational changes to support the effort. The likelihood of this sort of "bottom up" request being granted can be greatly improved by effective communication channels, and by frequent first-hand experience with the change effort by those outside the changing unit.

A person or group should be identified within both the change unit and the larger organization to manage this interface. This frequently is done by including a member of top management

---

[4]Richard E. Walton, *The Diffusion of New Work Structures: Explaining Why Success Didn't Take*, Organizational Dynamics (New York: Amacom, 1975).

who does not work directly in the change area on the committee guiding the change, or by identifying a top management liaison who calls periodic joint meetings between the changing unit and top management to ensure understanding and support.

COORDINATOR

When companies introduce a new product, they appoint a product manager to attend to the guiding of the product through the required steps to become part of the established product line. Change efforts also need a product manager. The title ranges from "internal consultant" to "facilitator" to "coordinator." This person does not usurp management's role of providing leadership and direction. Rather, this person works closely with the stakeholders as a project manager or account executive. The role is to provide a central point for daily coordination.

In some organizations, the coordinator reports to the head of the core group or to the steering committee. This may not be appropriate in your organization, because of career path issues, rewards, evaluations, and similar items. Because the effort needs to be seen as line management's responsibility, if it is to become a way of life, it usually is best if the coordinator reports to a line manager, rather than to a human resources manager.

The coordinator plays an active role in working with all parties, and he or she often assumes a role similar to that of an external consultant—as a strategist and third-party helper when problems or conflicts arise.

Some training will be necessary to help the coordinator function effectively. Visiting other corporations, attending consulting skills seminars, and working with outside consultants are methods for such training.

The coordinator is often the first person to notice how well the effort is going. For this reason, he or she can be a resource for committees to get feedback on progress.

Although it may be easy for the various committees to delegate the implementation of team activities to the coordinator, the end result will be very little commitment on the part of line managers.

Therefore, management must ensure that the coordinator does not end up with all the responsibility and work.

Management is responsible for implementation. If the effort is seen as something done by the coordinator or the human resources function, those effected will accept little responsibility for it. If it is a joint effort, managers and union officials must see it as part of their ongoing daily responsibilities.

LEARNING CURVE

The ability of organization members to learn how to implement changes is related to their first-hand experience with the change effort. Organizations often assume that the work they have done in the initial change area will be understood by all, so expanding the effort to other parts of the organization is merely a simple progression. However, people who have not been actively involved in the initial effort will have a different level of acceptance, understanding, and ability to implement.

To assume that these people are ready to implement a team-based organization underestimates the magnitude of the type of change being undertaken. Consequently, expanding frequently requires replicating the initial groundwork in the new parts of the organization. Although some learning will take place, based upon observation, the people now being called on to implement must gain first-hand experience by going through the process themselves and learning as it evolves.

Employees who have introduced teams successfully in one part of the organization can help to implement them in other parts, as long as the authority, ownership, and responsibility of the managers and employees in the new areas are not undermined. Help should come in the form of consultation and helping employees to learn new skills. As a learning experience in some organizations, managers, union officials, and employees from the next area to undertake change have attended team meetings and similar skill-gathering sessions and learned from the implementation efforts that preceded theirs.

RESOURCES AND EXPANSION

Now consider the level of ongoing activity the organization can maintain prior to expanding a team effort in one area of the organization to other areas or increasing team responsibilities. The organization does not benefit by overtaxing its resources and, thereby, contributing to failure. However, going too slowly can appear to be the result of low commitment. The balance between overtaxing resources and going too slowly is a judgment call.

Depending on the type of change activity undertaken and how rapidly it is expanded, a resource crunch might occur. For example, starting teams requires training and facilitation, employee time off the job, and meeting space. Starting too many teams at once obviously will tax your resources.

Change efforts always will need resources to initiate and maintain them; they will not function by themselves. Perpetuating and expanding involvement activities is no different than expanding a management-by-objectives program. If teams are not continually maintained and provided with resources, they do not become a way of life.

Initially, change efforts do not run themselves, although, as they become part of a line manager's daily responsibility, they become more a way of operating and less of an extra effort. As teams mature, the resources required to initiate them can be reduced and deployed in new areas. The extent of reduction will have to be determined for each area, but certainly the time and energy of the consultant, coordinator, training resources, and the like can be reduced in the initial start-up area.

Self-managing or autonomous work teams encourage autonomy and self-governing behaviors. As these new behaviors become a way of life, the resources needed to maintain them can be reduced and reallocated to other parts of the organization.

Expansion requires development of new skills by everyone. Training will be needed for newly hired and transferred employees. The training role that initially may have been supplied by outside sources should be assumed by internal coordinators and facilitators or by the training department.

Some organizations have established a transition manager who works on the big picture, planning and assuring that the change strategy is working.[5] This could be the coordinator or a member of the core group or of the steering committee. This person or group constantly evaluates the current status and future direction of the effort.

The transition manager, along with management and the union, should review planned organization changes. The purpose is to determine that they are done in a way that is consistent with the philosophy of management.

After consulting approximately one year with an organization, its coordinator informed me of a meeting its steering committee had, which was to plan a major change effort in the work processes of a department. At the end of the planning session, as everyone was about to leave, the coordinator said, "We have just planned a major change and have not involved those affected." All members present agreed and returned to the room to develop plans to solicit employee input on how the change should be made.

This type of thinking must be built into the everyday processes of the organization. Without it, decisions will be made that may undermine the new way of operating.

PERPETUATING (Becoming a Way of Life)

Management should look constantly for opportunities to make the planned changes a way of life. Changing the organization structure, policies, systems, and procedures to support teams, signals to employees that teams are not a fad and will continue. As teams function and experience success, pressures are exerted to change the way the organization does business to accommodate increased teamwork and team autonomy. Attention must be

---

[5]Richard Beckhard and Reuben T. Harris, *Organizational Transitions; Managing Complex Change* (Reading, Mass.: Addison-Wesley Publishing, 1977).

paid to these pressures and then improvements made to incorporate the types of change needed.

In a manufacturing organization, the engineering procedure was changed to include those assembling the product in a review of the process before it is finalized. In effect, the engineering team was expanded to include assemblers. The planning procedure of a research organization was changed to include all functions that come into contact with a new product within the product planning team.

Attention to incorporating the positive aspects of teams into daily routines is key to making them standard practice. Occasionally, organizations either explicitly or implicitly take the position that, if the change is good, it will just happen. However, successful efforts do not just happen—they are the result of hard work and attention to detail. The managers of many organizations devote time during their weekly meetings to discussing how to improve teamwork within the organization.

RECOGNIZING TEAMWORK

All opportunities should be taken to recognize good team performance. The recognition acts as a boost and energizer. It can take many forms, such as letters and personal recognition for jobs well done or team presentations to top management on problems it has solved. The management and union hierarchy continually must reinforce the changes by rewarding people who actively contribute. For example, when managers are rewarded for developing teams, it gives a clear signal to the organization that team development is an important and necessary part of increasing employee contribution and organization effectiveness.

DOCUMENTATION

Documenting the vision and management philosophy can help ensure that new managers are aware of the new way of operating and will not arbitrarily implement an inconsistent approach.

Early in this book, we described organizations as being in a stable state, meaning they have policies, procedures, and ways of operating that tend to perpetuate stability.[6] To ensure lasting change, the new way of operating must be stabilized, requiring many of the same stabilizing factors as the old organization—for example, policies and procedures. Policies should be stabilizers and not deterrents to new ways of operating. New policies will have to stand the test of continual challenge and evolution.

To perpetuate the improvements realized through teams, the positive outcomes must be institutionalized. New decision-making and communications processes that are beneficial must be formalized into standard operating procedures. Structures as simple as weekly meetings, committees, advisory groups, review panels, and conferences are ways to encourage and perpetuate teamwork.

PROVIDING TIME AND OPPORTUNITY

Management's role is to help teams find the time to meet, make decisions, plan, and so on. Maintaining an effective change effort is similar to maintaining your lawn—that is, if teams and committees do not meet on a regular basis to discuss how they are doing, much like your lawn, they grow wild or become less effective. It is difficult to find time for meetings in a three-shift continuous operation. Many organizations have teams meeting on overtime. In some organizations, employees voluntarily come in either 15 minutes before or stay after shift for meetings.

In addition to regular cross-shift and team meetings, time and opportunity must be available to assess the present ways of operating and to try new ones. Teams and committees must have opportunities to assess how they are doing and redirect their efforts.

In many organizations, this takes the form of monthly or quarterly meetings to evaluate present efforts and determine future directions. Periodic team self-assessment meetings can help to re-

---

[6]Donald Schon, *Beyond the Stable State* (New York: Random House, 1971).

generate enthusiasm by eliminating blocks to effective teamwork. These meetings provide the team the time and opportunity to discuss teamwork issues that often do not surface during the short and often hurried daily meetings.

FEEDBACK AND REPLANNING

After six months to a year, and at least yearly thereafter, key leaders of the change should spend several hours away from telephones and interruptions to critique the progress and discuss the future direction of the change effort. The following questions should be explored after soliciting feedback from all levels of the organization on how the effort is going.

1. Is the change effort successfully affecting the following?
   - Product or service quality.
   - Organizational effectiveness.
   - Job satisfaction.
2. What are the implications of continuing on the present course for future product or service quality, for organizational effectiveness, and for employee job satisfaction?
3. Are we satisfied with the present direction and projected future direction of the change? If not, what changes are required?
4. What changes, practices, and behaviors have proven successful and how do we increase and perpetuate them?
5. What systems, policies, processes, and daily operating procedures should be altered to increase team support and make teamwork a way of life?
6. Are adequate resources available?
7. What behaviors positively impact upon the change effort? What rewards are needed to support and perpetuate them?
8. What behaviors negatively impact upon the change effort, and how do we eliminate or reduce their influence?

The end result of the meeting should be a clearer direction over the next six months. It is not necessary to have a clear image for the year; that may not occur. If it does, great! Sometimes you only know short-term direction; however, as the image emerges, it should be communicated as broadly as possible.

The value of feedback is the replanning it allows. Feedback from all levels should be a way of life, resulting in continual change and fine-tuning. Without it, there is no self-correction mechanism within the organization.

The objective is evolution, with enough stability to maintain personal and organizational effectiveness—not revolution. Evolution happens when continual feedback exists, which leads to replanning and redirection. Revolution happens when communications are cut off and there is no feedback, and management does not understand what employees want. Without constant feedback, there is no way to determine whether those involved value and support the change.

Feedback should be used to plan and not be used as a "report card." When a need arises to report back to corporate management, reports should be informal, rather than a long written justification of actions and results. Organizations should be careful not to overmeasure or overcontrol the effort and, thereby, stifle the experimentation, creativity, and risk-taking required to change existing norms and operating procedures.

A common mistake is to measure activity, such as the number of teams, rather than their impact. The overall goals and success in achieving them should be the basis for measurement. Several types of feedback should be considered.

Interviews

Interviews should include a random and representative sample of employees from all levels of the organization. Interviews with team members or exit interviews with people rotating off teams can be informative. Interviews should focus on their experiences in the team, suggestions for improvement, and whether change is indeed transferring to the everyday work environment. (See in the appendix, the Employee Participation Interview.) Sometimes staff groups and outside suppliers or customers can provide perceptions of the effectiveness of the changes within the organization.

The feedback from interviews is most useful when summarized into major themes. The results should be fed back to employees, and their ideas for improvement should be solicited. Their responses should help shape and be closely tied to actions taken to improve.

Surveys

Gathering feedback through questionnaires concerning the organization's strengths, weaknesses, causal factors, and opportunities for action can be helpful. The information obtained can be analyzed and communicated to the various planning committees and employees, so action plans can be developed and implemented.

One organization yearly assesses how the team effort is progressing. All employees complete a questionnaire. The results are tabulated and fed back to the total organization. Employees and management can make recommendations for changes. A management committee reviews the recommendations and plans for the needed changes.

Be careful that surveys are not too extensive and overwhelm the organization with data that cannot be effectively acted upon.

It is best to create several information collection and feedback mechanisms—for example, interviews, surveys, what's-on-your-mind question and answer meetings, suggestion programs, grievance reports, and exit interviews. They should be looked at regularly. The emphasis is on active response to data, rather than on scorekeeping.

TIMETABLES

Timetables should be general and flexible, to guide the process and provide targets. To have direction is more important than to meet specific dates. It is very difficult to plan and predict where the change effort will be at any point in time. Too many factors, such as employee acceptance and the need for organization-wide systems changes, can affect the overall timing.

Organizations that force dates, because these have been established, will hurry the process and not involve people to the extent they should to get the needed acceptance and understanding. Consequently, they may get lip service and perfunctory involvement.

The most frequent problem is best exemplified by the example of one top management group which took months to decide what it wanted and how to involve the union and employees. Since the group was now months behind its planned startup date, it decided that a quick meeting with the union and a memo to all employees would bring everyone up to date and it could launch teams.

As the consultant to the group, I said that this might be rushing the employee and union acceptance of the change. A long discussion ensued, during which it was pointed out that employees and the union might need some time and the opportunity to understand and buy into the changes just as they had. The result was a replanning of the appropriate steps to ensure understanding and acceptance and a revised schedule to accommodate what was needed versus what was initially planned. This type of adaptive planning, as was pointed out at the beginning of this book, is a key to successful efforts.

SUMMARY

As teams develop and are given more autonomy, the manager's role shifts from one-on-one manager to team leader and boundary manager. These roles emphasize teaching, planning, coordinating, and resource allocation.

In addition to focusing their attention on the team, managers should be alert for needed changes in the organization's work process to make them supportive of teams.

Managers must establish mechanisms for constant feedback from the teams. Feedback is necessary for the continual learning and replanning that are essential to a successful change effort. Chapter Ten will further elaborate on the key elements of a successful evolution to a team-based organization.

APPENDIX

Coordinator's Qualifications

The qualifications or characteristics the coordinator should possess are listed in priority order. It is unlikely that one individual will possess all of these characteristics.

- Recognized as competent in present job.
- Committed, enthusiastic, and believes in the philosophies underlying team-based organizations.
- Viewed as impartial and able to work with the union, employees, and management.
- Good interpersonal and communications skills—written and oral.
- Good analytical and problem-solving skills.
- Able to identify issues and take constructive action with minimal direction.
- Has group facilitation skills and knowledge of how to bring about change. These skills and knowledge can be acquired through training, working with a consultant, and experience.

Coordinator's Responsibilities

The coordinator's responsibilities in other organizations have included the following functions:

1. Being the central resource for information and for coordinating and developing steering committee communications, including newsletters, bulletin boards, and the like.

2. Serving as internal consultant.

3. Maintaining records, gathering data to evaluate the effort's effectiveness, developing status reports.

4. Acting as liaison between the external consultant and the organization.

5. Coordinating the resources required to launch and maintain participation activities.

6. Working with the various committees to arrange for necessary resources, such as staff personnel, to assist with problem-solving groups, obtaining external resources, preparation of budget requests, and similar matters.

7. In conjunction with the training department and the external consultant, identifying orientation and training needs, and, if skilled, helping develop and administer and conduct the required training programs.

8. Providing guidance to managers, employees, and union.

Facilitator's Responsibilities

As teams are starting up, some organizations have found it necessary to have facilitators. Facilitators primarily are responsible for the "care and feeding" of participative activities within a given area. They may have a dotted or solid line relationship to the coordinator. Their job is much like the coordinator's but more limited in the area covered and the scope of responsibility.

They primarily are concerned with the effective functioning of teams within their area. Some organizations have trained their supervisors to be facilitators.

Typical responsibilities for a facilitator include the following functions:

- Assisting in launching team activities.
- Coordinating and scheduling employee training.
- Facilitating initial team meetings to ensure their smooth operations.
- Providing daily support by observing and facilitating teams.
- Ensuring that communications strategies are working.
- Arranging for engineering, quality control, and other resources to meet with teams to provide assistance, as necessary.

Employee Participation Interview

Employee interviews can be helpful in assessing how well team efforts are being implemented and how they should be altered. The following are examples of the types of questions you might want to ask:

1. Tell me briefly what your job is.
2. How have you been involved in team efforts?
3. How has participation on a team affected you?
4. What do you see as the positive/negative outcomes of your participation on a team regarding:

- Relationship with:
    Supervisor.
    Peers.
    Other departments.
    Customers.
- Involvement in decisions affecting your work.
- Improvement in work environment.
- Communications.
- Involvement in planning or goal-setting.
- Other.

5. How is your team doing?
    a. Is the team addressing the subjects you think they should? Why or why not?
    b. If not, what should they address?
    c. If not, what prevents the team from addressing these subjects?

6. To what extent do management and the union support participation on a team? How is their support or lack of support demonstrated?

7. To what extent do employees support teamwork?

8. What forces are working for or against a higher level of teamwork?

9. To what extent is teamwork integrated into everyday activities? Give examples.

10. Where do you see the greatest leverage for teams to improve organizational effectiveness and employee job satisfaction.

11. What is your vision of what teams should be doing two years from now?

12. If you had a magic wand, how would you like to be more involved to improve your personal job satisfaction and how effectively you perform your job?

13. Other comments.

14. Questions.

Chapter Ten

Keys to Success

O ne of the first questions I am asked frequently by new clients is, "How do we make the change to greater utilization of teams?" My answer as consultant is, "It depends," and I describe a long list of issues, like the nature of the work, past cultural biases, and similar items. It usually only takes a few seconds before their eyes glaze and they seem to be thinking about anything but what I am saying.

Frequently, what they expected was a magic formula and they didn't receive it. There are no magic formulas. There are, however, key factors that underlie the successes seen to date.

These factors were identified in Chapter One and elaborated on throughout the book, including suggested ways to incorporate them into your change effort.

The following is a summary of these five factors and how they can influence your change effort.

ORGANIZATIONAL GOALS AND CHANGE STRATEGY CONGRUENCE

- **The change strategy must fit with the organization's business strategy and goals.** Developing teams in a business that requires teamwork and coordination is congruent. Developing teams in a business that requires individual performance versus teamwork is not congruent.

Where organizations see teams as a way of addressing critical business issues, they find time for and support teamwork. Sometimes organizations have to be in crisis before they perceive a need to do something different. To be hoped is that more and more organizations will ask, "How can we get better?" If one of the answers is better use of teams, then "teams" fit with the organization's change strategy.

The following quote from an executive exemplifies the congruence between organizational goals and their strategy for managing human resources.

> Teams are a way of managing the business. For years we managed the numbers, now we are managing people and they manage the numbers.

• **There is organization-wide application of the strategy versus isolated pockets.** As systems begin to change to support teams, they become less congruent with the parts of the organization that have not changed. It is difficult and cumbersome to maintain two sets of systems. Maintaining information and decision-making systems that support teams and treat people equally, along with a perquisite system that differentiates based on level, seems out of synch to employees and gives a dual message.

MANAGEMENT, UNION, AND EMPLOYEE SUPPORT

• **There is support at all levels, with local support being particularly important.** At Ford Motor Credit, the chairman and the president were active participants in the steering committee. Local branch managers also were key in implementing successful efforts in their field operations. Strong management and union support—demonstrated by active participation on committees, by giving supportive speeches, and by helping to resolve issues— was crucial to Ford Motor Company's and the UAW's early efforts in employee involvement.

• **There is a long-term orientation to change.**   Ford Motor Company recognized that the changes it undertook in the early 80s would take years.

• **A timely response is given to all teams, regardless of the size of the issue.**   Employees are kept informed of future plans and are told why their recommendations have or have not been implemented.

• **There is a willingness on the part of management, the union, and employees to experiment with new ways of working together.**   Ford and the UAW set up forums for the purpose of talking about new ways of working in an environment that would support experimentation.

• **Adequate resources are made available to support teams and to implement recommended changes.**   Time is made available for the training of teams and managers and for team meetings. Finding time for teams to meet to coordinate their activities in a 24-hour continuous operation is difficult but essential for an effective team.

• **Employees trust management and are willing to work with the managers to bring about the changes.**   Employees are patient. They do not expect things to improve overnight. Several organizations that used problem-solving teams as their initial change effort later experienced frustration from employees when the team's recommendations were not quickly implemented. Management had to explain the complexity of implementing some of the recommendations before employees were satisfied that they weren't just dragging their feet.

Using team meetings to update employees on the progress of various recommendations or projects also can help set realistic expectations about how long it takes to make changes.

• **People work hard to make team meetings and teams work.**   In some successful efforts, employees come to team meetings on their day off; others come in before or after the shift on their own time.

LEADERSHIP

• **Key managers provide leadership by advocating a clear, constant vision and by actively participating in the change process.**   In one client organization, the plant manager keeps a constant focus on the vision. All decisions and new directions are constantly tested against it.

• **There are proactive strong committees that provide direction and help.**   Steering, design, and implementation committees increase the opportunity for more managers and employees to help create and direct the change. These committees spread the responsibility and increase the number of people who are committed to the change.

• **Internal consultants are available, trained, and expected to take an active role in keeping the change effort moving ahead.**   In many divisions of GTE, the success of its employee participation efforts can be partly attributed to the diligence of its internal consulting staff, which trains, consults, and provides coordinating support.

• **There are good team leaders who are trained to work with teams as facilitators and coaches.**   Over and over again there are examples of teams doing well because they have good coaches.

• **A feeling of family is created by organization-wide activities.**   Such activities include newsletters, social gatherings, sports events, and charitable drives. Employees feel good about their accomplishments together. In one organization, employees provided the leadership to donate the profits from company vending machines to charity.

PLANNED ADAPTIVE APPROACH

• **The application of the change is flexible.**   The planning and implementation of change is done with flexibility rather than with a rigid adherence to pre-established guidelines and timetables. While interviewing a manager involved in an effort that was labeled "less successful," the manager described how he watched as teams floundered, because the guidelines he was given said he should not direct the teams. In organizations where the efforts were labeled "successful," managers stepped in to provide direction when they felt it was needed.

• **There are frequent departmental or total unit meetings for business information, two-way exchange, and problem-solving.**   Without feedback, problems do not surface rapidly for resolution. This can result in rigid adherence to a plan and turned-off employees who may feel more like undermining instead of supporting the effort.

KNOWLEDGE AND SKILLS

• **Everyone has the knowledge and skills necessary to perform their job.**   Considerable training supported the more successful efforts. The type of training fell into four categories of skills: job skills, interpersonal skills, team skills, and management skills.

THE FUTURE OF TEAMS

Organizations are using teams to perform all aspects of an operation. Teams are coordinating and managing what was at one time the province of staff functions. Teams are receiving materials, manufacturing the product or providing the service, shipping the product, and interacting with suppliers and customers. They are assuming much of the work of staff groups, such as financial analysis, quality testing, and hiring.

Certainly there are implications for the role of functional and staff groups as teams assume more responsibility. In some organizations, these groups have been reduced in size. How the functional expertise will be maintained and progress is an issue that organizations will need to address. It is likely that teams will do the more common tasks, and staff groups will continue to do the more complex and cutting-edge work.

Teams offer a unit with which employees can identify. Working closely on a day-to-day basis with others can forge strong ties to each member and to the team. While this can be a positive force for commitment, productivity, and job satisfaction, it also can have two major downside risks.

One, as environmental demands change, new teams may need to form. Employees may find difficulty in changing teams and leaving old alliances. Two, each team usually feels it is the best.

Such a team occasionally likes to prove this by competing with other teams. While competition can be healthy, it can also have negative consequences if one team's success affects another's ability to perform.

A financial service organization's team design exemplifies these two potential problems. The firm has 12 teams that provide service via phone to customers. Each team has a specific set of customers. However, as one team's work load exceeds its capacity to handle the load, the phone call rolls over to other teams. If the other team chooses to maximize its productivity, it could either transfer the calls or not answer them. Furthermore, as new clients are added to or dropped from the overall company portfolio, teams will have to be restructured by adding or deleting members. As you can see, each team is interdependent with the others.

This organization is taking several steps to facilitate the movement of team members and to ensure that competition does not result in one team prospering at the other's expense. The firm is training each team and emphasizing the use of similar work processes by all teams, thus making it easier to switch teams. The firm also is providing information and tools that are used with all clients to each team. Finally, the firm is setting some goals by client, which are specific to the client. But the firm is also setting total company production, quality, and other goals. It is rewarding teams on the basis of overall organizational performance. They want to avoid rewarding teams in a way that might cause less cooperation between them. They want to maintain a total organization focus by all teams.

As new demands are placed on team-based organizations, will

they be able to perform or will new types of organizations emerge? I suspect both will occur.

Anybody who has ever engaged in a problem-solving activity, where, first, individuals answer a number of questions and then, using consensus, answer them as a team, will remember that, providing the team used good problem-solving and meeting processes, the team score was better than the average individual score. Proving you can add to an old adage: That two heads are better than one—and that there will always be a place in organizations for teamwork.

Probably, some pendulum-swinging will apply to and from the use of teams. However, I believe the basic principles that underlie teams will survive, be practiced in many forms, and will help organizations prosper. They are:

- Empowering employees to perform work.
- Collaborating to coordinate and accomplish tasks.
- Continuing employee commitment through participation in goal setting, planning, and decision making.

TEAMS—A CONTINUOUS PROCESS

This book has outlined many of the issues to be addressed, and it has provided guidelines and practical first steps in establishing a team-based organization. Each organization is unique, and managers will need to adapt the ideas that seem relevant to fit their needs.

Making these changes takes time; it is a continuous process, not a one-shot quick fix. Naisbitt in his book *Megatrends* says, "You can't change unless you completely rethink what it is you are doing, unless you have a wholly new vision."[1]

---

[1] John Naisbitt, *Megatrends* (New York: Warner Books, 1982).

Moving to a team-based organization requires the creation of a clear vision and frequently a restructuring of how the organization functions. This can take years and require extraordinary effort and persistence.

The frustrations of reaching your vision are guaranteed to be many. However, as some organizations are finding, the rewards can surpass them.

Good luck!

Index

Hackman, J. Richard, 105, 111
Hanna, David P., 103, 109
Harris, Reuben T., 14, 53 n, 144 n
Hays, Brian, 7 n
Hierarchical (formal; functional; traditional) organizations, vii, 2, 24, 82
  advantages of, 42–43
  disadvantages of, 42
  primary design of, 83
  shortcomings, 83
  structure, 86
Hierarchy of team(s), 97
High involvement, and change effort, 37–40
High Involvement Management (Lawler), 7
Hirschhorn, Larry, viii n

Implementation committee
  membership, 94–95
  role, 93–94
  size, 94
  voluntary versus required participation, 94–95
Information
  as design factor, 111
  planning questions, 117
  "privileged" information, 46
  systems for employees, 46
Interdependence
  analysis of Questionnaire, 14–18, 19
  as design factor, 110
  determining per-change status, 14–18, 19
  impact on change effort, 20
  impact on where-to-start, 71
  management of, 14
  Questionnaire, 15–18
Internal consultant; *see* Coordinator
Interviews, as feedback tool, 148–49

Job satisfaction, and teams, 19, 47, 161
Job significance, as design factor, 112

Key manager
  definition, 53
  as initiator of change, 54
  leadership role, 158
Keys to success, of team-based organizations, 9–11, 155–62
Kimberly Clark, ix
Knowledge, as major key to success, 11, 159

Lawler, Edward E., III, ix n, 7–8, 25, 26 n, 37, 44

Leadership
  continuum of, 136–39
  as major key to success, 11, 158
Leading a team-based organization, 133–51
  analysis of own leadership, 139
  coordinator; *see* Coordinator
  documentation, 145–46
  feedback and replanning, 147–49
  interface with larger system, 139–41
  leadership continuum, 136–39
  learning curve during change effort, 142
  manager(s) role, 133–34
  one-on-one manager, 135
  perpetuating the change effort, 144–45
  providing time and opportunity, 146–47
  recognition for teamwork, 145
  resources and expansion, 143–44
  team boundary manager, 136
  Team Leadership Continuum, 136–39
  team leader(s) role, 134–36
  timetables, 149–50
Ledford, Gerald, Jr., 31
Letter of understanding, 65
Long-term orientation, and change effort, 39–40
LTV Steel, 3

McGregor, Douglas, 25 n
McGregor's Theory Y, 25
Management
  complacency as problem, 33
  of interdependence, 14
  knowledge as key to success, 11, 159
  philosophy questions, 116
  skills as key factor, 11, 159
  startup concerns, 56–57
  support as key factor, 10–11
Management-by-objectives, 143
Management/union interaction
  broader scope of access and information, 46
  Ford Motor Company/UAW experience, 61, 63
  letter of understanding, 65
  moratorium on prior agreements, 63
Manager(s)
  boundary manager, 136
  concerns about change, 56–57, 134
  and documentation, 145–46
  key manager; *see* Key manager
  one-on-one manager, 135
  performance reviewed by employees, 48
  resistance to change effort, reasons for, 58
  rewards system for, 45

Also Available from BUSINESS ONE IRWIN:

FIRING ON ALL CYLINDERS
The Service/Quality System for High-Powered Corporate Performance
Jim Clemmer
with Barry Sheehy and Achieve International/Zenger-Miller Associates
Gives you a detailed and practical map for improving service and quality in your organization. Outlines Achieve International's Service/Quality System that is used by dozens of public and private sector companies, such as American Express, IBM-Canada, Black & Decker, and many others. Clemmer shows how to integrate three formerly separate organizational performance fields to improve your overall business strategy.
ISBN: 1-55623-704-9 $29.95

SECOND TO NONE
How Our Smartest Companies Put People First
Charles Garfield
A Main Selection of The Executive Program
Discover how you can create a workplace where both people and profits flourish! Charles Garfield, the best-selling author of Peak Performers, gives you an inside look at today's leading businesses and how they became masters at expanding the teamwork and creativity of their workforce. Using his unique mix of practical strategies gleaned from our smartest companies, he shows how you can provide superior service to your customers, maintain a competitive edge during times of rapid transition, and inspire innovation, partnership, and total participation from your employees and managers.
ISBN: 1-55623-360-4 $22.95

SELF-DIRECTED WORK TEAMS
The New American Challenge
Jack D. Orsburn, Linda Moran, Ed Musselwhite, and John H. Zenger
Show employees from diverse areas of your company how to work together more efficiently so your firm can compete more effectively! Includes case histories from TRW, Cummins Engine, General Electric, Blue Cross of Ohio, Hughes Tool, and many others.
ISBN: 1-55623-341-8 $39.95

BEING THE BOSS
The Importance of Leadership and Power
Abraham L. Gitlow
Discover the best ways to lead a corporate team so you can minimize internal conflict and improve morale. Gitlow shows how you can exercise power and authority to gain improved productivity, increased profits, and more satisfied employees and stockholders.
ISBN: 1-55623-635-2 $24.95

KIN CARE AND THE AMERICAN CORPORATION
Solving the Work/Family Dilemma
Dayle M. Smith
Smith shows how corporations can solve some of their staffing problems—including high turnover, absenteeism, recruiting failure, and declining productivity. Includes valuable checklists, forms, and guidelines you can use to determine the best programs.
ISBN: 1-55623-449-X $24.95

THE DOMINO EFFECT
How to Grow Sales, Profits, and Market Share through Super Vision
Donald J. Vlcek and Jeffrey P. Davidson
Details the proven techniques Domino's Pizza uses to target and maintain a 50% annual growth goal. This unique, behind-the scenes look reveals how virtually any company can efficiently implement the same winning management strategies.
ISBN: 1-55623-602-6 $24.95

All prices quoted are in U.S. currency and are subject to change without notice. Availalble at fine bookstores and libraries everywhere.